THE BATTLE OF BRITAIN

AND

OTHER SHORT STORIES

by
Arthur J. McChrystal, Brigadier General, US, ret.

WARM SPRINGS PRESS
TUCSON, AZ

The Battle of Britain and Other Short Stories

ISBN: 978-0-578-66008-0

Cover photo from McChrystal family archives.
Editing, cover and page design by Karen McChrystal

WARM SPRINGS PRESS
TUCSON, AZ.

CONTENTS

1. Early Days in Eureka, Utah   5

2. The Ninety-Day Wonder   17

3. Nine and Out   23

4. Old China Hand   37

5. The Battle of Britain   63

6. Don't Gild the Lily   107

7. March Murders   111

8. Leakage   113

9. The Making of a Spy   115

10. Medals, Anyone?   121

11. The 17-Minute Surrender   127

12. Michie Ran a Bar   133

13. The Canadian Safari   137

Photos   145

Biography   165

1. EARLY DAYS IN EUREKA, UTAH

Two different tribes responded to the "Go West, young man" plea of Horace Greeley. One was the Robbins family from Indiana in the early eighties, headed by Grandfather Robbins. With his wife, of the Adamson Clan, daughter Isabella Robbins, later to be my mother, and two boys David and Box, they traveled to Utah. Skirting Salt Lake City, the party moved to fertile farming lands near Gunnison, Utah and settled there. The McChrystal family had started from northern Michigan at approximately the same time, with Grandfather John Henry McChrystal at the helm, with his wife Sarah Hancock McChrystal (possible descendent of John Hancock), together with sons John Hancock McChrystal (my father, Jackson; Mark; Noah; and Jason; and daughters Sarah and Annie). The McChrystals headed for the hills and the miners' Tintic District, 7000 feet high in the Wasatch, between Utah Lake on one side and Utah Valley on the other, approximately 100 miles south of Salt Lake City.

Experienced in mining in Michigan, John's main objective was capital. This came in the person of John Quincy Adams Packard, who put in hundreds of thousands and pulled out a few million.

Among the original mines owned by the McChrystals were the Gemini, with 37 miles of workings to a depth of 1800 feet, the last 500 being under water; Eagle; and Blue Belle. There was also Godiva, high on the hills towards Knightsville, named after famous Mormon Jesse Knight. The family also owned Tintic Mercantile Co., directly across from Salt Lake Route Station.

With money, know-how and drive, Eureka started to boom. Vigilantes worked out on "Molly McGuires," radicals from Pennsylvania. They also discouraged unsportsmanlike conduct, such as five aces, by hanging transgressors from an old head frame on Upper Church St., which street also featured 21 saloons.

Grandfather McChrystal was the accepted leader of both town and family. In 1896 a flood roared down Tintic Creek, threatening the Bullion Beck shaft. Grandfather McChrystal actively aided in placing sand bags around the shaft's collar until miners were rescued, then he died from a heart attack. He was buried in Salt Lake City. Mining operations continued under direction of my father, John H. and his brother, Jackson, with Alex taking over the Tintic Mercantile. He had graduated in Medicine from Pennsylvania but never practiced.

Originally the McChrystals were The Establishment in Eureka, then in moved the Walter Fitches, who purchased our Gemini mine and other holdings. With the death of my father, John H. McChrystal during the flu epidemic of 1920 and gradual working out of the mines, interest turned toward the Fitch holdings. Later, approximately 1914, a valuable discovery was made some twenty miles north of the district by Radditz, and Eureka gradually became a ghost town. To prove my mental incapacity for finance we did the original assaying for the Tintic Standard, knew what they had, bought their stock for some ten cents a share, and cagily sold out for eighty cents, later to see the stock go to some twenty dollars a share.

Tex Wilson, bad man of the West, had some four killings to his credit. Released from the Provo Insane Asylum, he had an idea that my Grandfather John H. had cheated him out of some mining property, and threatened his life. His abode was a stone and brush shack on the outskirts of town, avoided by everyone. With the death of my grandfather, Tex transferred his interest and threats to my father. Around 1902 we were living below the Godiva Mine, between Eureka and Knightsville. Tex Wilson, fully armed with heavy pistol, knocked at the door. My father departed out to the corral and mounted a fast horse. My mother opened the door. Tex remarked to me, "Kid, a'hm a goin' to kill yer Paw!"

Mother meantime invited him in for a coffee, saying that John K. had been called out of town. When I started to point out that he was just leaving the corral, I got a fast slap.

Some years later, around 1914, Tex had killed another man, but was again released from the asylum, reportedly coming to Eureka. Father was in Salt Lake, so my two uncles, Mark and Alex; Chris Erickson, an old gambler who taught me to play poker; and myself were a welcoming committee when the noon Salt Lake Route train backed into the station.

We were all armed, myself with my favorite weapon, a long-barreled pistol. Passengers dismounted, but no Tex. A slow march through the train, weapons drawn, revealed Tex in the baggage car, where he had over stimulated himself and was snoring on the floor.

We bound him carefully. I got a mild Mickey from my saloon, and Tex was returned to Salt Lake as Dead Freight, never to be heard of again.

The family poker game was traditional ... the McChrystal clan, Paw, Ma, sister Frances and son Arthur (named after the Round Table), with visiting guests. The latter invariably failed to notice an old antique mirror, directly back of the guest's seat, that cast reflections, also information, on the visitor's hands. This often resulted in the guest leaving minus a few ounces of gold dust. The usual courtesy of supplying the guest with carfare home was unnecessary, as the ancestral home was high on the hill. Gravity, plus a couple of slugs of Old Painkiller, was sufficient to bring him to Lower Main Street, where he would be either arrested for loitering or run over by a loaded ore wagon.

Time to Go Further West

From the mountain fastnesses of Central Utah, in 1906, the McChrystal clan prepared to set out for California. This included

John Jr. the father, mom Issa, sister Fran and her family. They were fed up with everything – too much work, too much wind, too many neighboring relatives. At the time when a hundred grand was a tidy chunk of dough, the clan was reasonably loaded.

Gathering together the family *"lares et penates,"* two leather-bound trunks, including a chunk of salted quartz that had enabled the paternal grandparent, John McChrystal, to sell a large portion of apparently worthless rock to an Easterner, John Q. Packard. To the surprise of Grandfather, this stuff turned out to be a winner.

The only transportation out of Eureka was rail, and after a few days' practice bending my knees under a seat, I was enabled to ride half-fare to Salt Lake, providing enough funds for us to eat.

My father was an inveterate subscriber to various periodicals, not including the sexy type. He had read a most attractive ad: "Be a Gentleman Farmer. Bask in the Soft Sunshine of Santa Clara Valley and Let Nature Do the Work." Smaller print disclosed that one of the particular wonders in this area, a mere fling from the City of the Golden Sun, was prunes.

While my father was generous to a fault, he was a bit challenged in the alimentary department, and the prospect of ample cheap prunes was fascinating.

So bag and baggage, Mom wearing her best cowhide-chinchilla wrap, Sister and I wearing our first pairs of shoes, and Dad resplendent in a Montgomery Ward Brooks Brothers dark blue suit, with an interesting tinge of green after exposure to the sun, clambered aboard the Southern Pacific Blitz, en route for San Francisco. Farewells were paid by weeping relatives plus a few creditors ... plus a couple shots. I thought they were farewell salutes until I noticed a hole in Pop's new derby.

Two days later and at least a half pound heavier from cinders and coal dust, we disembarked at Oakland for the Ferry trip. When I heard one waiting guest say to another "Look at that damn fairy!" I thought that we were to be towed piggy-back over the broad expanse of water. Pa explained that that was merely a dirty word and we were going on a boat.

At that time Dr. Alec McChrystal, graduate cum laude, of Pennsylvania, was a temporary resident in San Francisco due to a slight incident that happened in Eureka, Utah, a couple of years prior. A half-pregnant young lady had done a full gainer, falling from the roof of the Eureka Skyscraper, four stories, landing on Dennis J. O'Sullivan, portly proprietor of one of Eureka's 23 drinking establishments. This knocked loose his Knights of Columbus watch worn across his chest, inflicting, according to the *Eureka Reporter,* "painful impact contusions in the area of the 'charm'".

In the resultant confusion, Dr. McChrystal decided that the balmy air of San Francisco would not only be good for his health but would save him from the frustrated rage of Mrs. O'Sullivan, temporarily deprived of marital solace.

We were met by the distinguished doctor and taken to his palatial hotel residence on O'Farrell St., where they were not nosy about such things as names, marriage licenses and other formalities.

Two days later we were driven by the Barrett Livery Stable and Freight Handling Company down the majestic Road of Kings some fifty miles to the thriving village of Sunnyvale.

With the able assistance of the doctor, who had a real estate friend, we became the proud possessors of ten acres of prune orchard plus a small house with two turrets, at the end of a winding palm-shaded road, plus a high water tank and a huge single oak tree. It really seemed a paradise after the windswept heights of Eureka, even if we were not experienced farmers or fruit growers. Our first move was to add two more towers to the house and to arrange for a neighboring farmer to handle the fruit crop. How he carried this out was questionable. As I recall, the only return we had from the first season's crop was getting the boxes by freight, collect. Meantime Dad had purchased a Cadillac, that is, a locally altered chassis with seats for two in front and a place for three in back, reachable by a back entrance, that occasionally failed, dropping the passengers. We would chug along the El Camino Real, often as far as Mountain View, honking gaily at passing wagons and occasionally pausing to adjust the back seat ... or pick up ejected passengers. Except for dust, the only air pollutant came from the stacks of the nearby Hendy Iron Works.

However, our dream life began to fail. Dad developed rheumatism and was practically bed-ridden. To add to the general complications, St. Andreas foot-faulted early in the morning of April 18, 1906. The resulting San Francisco earthquake and fire swept the ground. Our two new house turrets tumbled to earth and Dad jumped out of bed to run the fastest hundred over broken ground ever recorded in the county.

The year following there was another type of earthquake, the Financial Crash of 1907, with prices of lead and silver dropping to all time lows, together with our family situation. We had to sell and go back to the mines, prunes or no prunes.

Back to the Mines in Eureka

I wasn't too happy at the welcome or lack of same when we returned. I also reached the firm conclusion that there was no percentage working for relatives. However, job openings in summer for twelve-year-olds were limited. So, swallowing both conviction and pride, I started as an assayer's helper at the Gemini, a family-owned mine, at a satisfactory wage of $1.50 per day. My boss was an old German, Frank Broehm, grizzled, hardboiled, and wonderful. In the morning we went underground with the early shift, picking up samples at various levels, starting with the 1800-foot station. Returning to the surface, using a 16-pound mallet we crushed, divided, and recrushed until the sample was reduced to an approximate 6 ounces. Then there was another operation, on a smooth iron plate with a rocker-shaped mallet sliding back and forth until we had the final result of a bare ounce of dust, ready for furnace melting and final steps to determine values per ton. It was monotonous but good for back muscles, useful in later life for glass lifting and martini drinking.

Frank and I had one thing in common – we were hopeful operators. When work shift was over we would catch up a couple of saddle horses and explore the wider neighborhood, seeking old abandoned mine workings, especially old assay office dumps. These often yielded small amounts of high-grade ore, and small profits.

Always looking for the Big Strike, one day we almost had it. It was an old abandoned working mine with a fairly deep shaft. The timbers were rotten. I slid down on a rope and found a peculiar formation near the bottom in a small drift. We sampled a vein thoroughly and returned late that night to the office. We crushed the samples and ran them through the furnace. Knocking off the slag from a lead button that remained, we melted the lead in bone-ash cupels, to find a smaller button. Gold, or both! Cooled, the button was placed on the assay scales, weighed delicately, then treated with acid to remove the silver. The scales showed an approximate value of $450 per ton in gold. But no silver ... that was worrisome.

We did another run with a new crucible, and this time got a positive result. Nothing! In our hurry we had grabbed a used crucible. At various times we had also done assays for small outfits with our assaying set-ups. We also did some work for the local dentist, melting up old dentures and annealing the gold, our charge being a little spillage plus $5.00 per ton. The used crucible had been used for golden teeth, "salting in reverse." [In mineral exploration, salting is the process of adding gold or silver to an ore sample to change the value of the ore with intent to deceive potential buyers of the mine.]

In the Fall I was sent to small private school in Salt Lake, All Hallows College, They had a good club bar and a small military unit. I became Captain of both.

That period was the start of my newspaper writing career, under Walter Bratz of the Salt Lake Telegram, writing about high school sports at the munificent payment of 25 cents per column inch. My initial story of an All Hallows victory over Eastside High involved a recital that should have netted $2.00. The Bratz re-write: "Saturday All Hallows beat Eastside 2 to 1." No pay for McChrystal.

It was the stories of Dan O. Jackling, copper king and millionaire, a friend of my father's, that made me dissatisfied with the $1.50 per day job. Also, there were tales of what had been dug out and also by-passed in the thirty-seven miles of working in the Old Gemini. This started me out on a lease that was to wind me up as a half owner of a saloon ... but more about that a bit later.

Naturally there were other important stages in my youth ... such as my first love affair. Among the evening attractions of Eureka was the "Star," a movie house with silent films, popcorn, and community singing from words flashed on the screen. "Sweet Adeline," "Old Apple Tree," were accompanied by the occasional flat note by the lady piano player. She was roughly twenty-nine, I an ambitious fifteen. I would slip away from my thirst-quenching duties at the saloon and sit enamored while she played. When not playing she wore long white gloves. I would take her home to her boarding house ... a brief interlude ... then back to the bar, starry-eyed and breathing heavily. I never even got her gloves off ... but God, how that girl could play.

The necessity of a formal education took me to Stanford in 1911, somewhat on the plutocratic side, as the income from the lease and my half of the saloon was running a neat five hundred dollars per month and no income tax.

My first three years studying mining engineering were comparatively uneventful. Rugby, of which I knew nothing, was being played at Stanford instead of football, so with fair success I devoted my athletic efforts to baseball and track.

Assisted by my alcohol/mineral income I was able to do a certain amount of social work, including buggy riding to such distant points as the Woodside Hermits, where the smart thing was to drink small glasses of sour red wine, hoping it would stimulate affairs or something. Actually, it was a very low quality wine.

With my senior year coming up, disaster struck. The lease had played out and "local option" had been voted in Juab County, Utah. No more bar, no more dough.

When I mentioned to my father that I would like to return to the halls of learning for my senior year, he casually inquired as to what I had done with my previous income. When I explained the drain caused by extra-mural activities, he smiled reminiscently and offered to pay transportation to Palo Alto, tuition, books and twenty-five dollars per month for living expenses.

I took the offer gladly, moved out of the Sigma Chi house and, with an equally poverty-stricken fraternity brother, set up housekeeping in a shack in the rear of a barn in Palo Alto. Here we learned domestic science and housekeeping the hard way. Did you ever sample apple sauce sandwiches? Or wait around the butcher shop until after closing time to get values?

Social opportunities were restricted, so we started on gainful projects. My partner had a job with a laundry and I checked over several opportunity ads, finally securing campus representation for two eastern firms. One was "Klassy Kustom Klogsil, well priced shoes for the Better Dressed." The other, as I recall it, was "Eastern College Clothes, a Madison Ave production for better-dressed campusites." Despite careful attention to instructions on the foot measuring device, shoes were apparently uncomfortable and just wouldn't break in. Repeat orders were negligible. Local tailor costs for alterations on the Campus Clothes led me to buy local yardage and use the local tailor, later applying the Campus labels. This cost me a few friends but was a money-maker.

Despite trials and inconveniences, the year was a success. I hit harder, jumped better, studied frantically, and graduated with a BA in Chemistry, I won a scholarship to the University of Utah, which gained me a MA in Metallurgy, plus some track fame, as the higher altitude helped my broad jumping.

Upon graduation in 1916, I went to the Bureau of Mines in Salt Lake to work on a "flotation" process, usable for previously-worked tailing dumps that still had reasonable metal values. This process, involving use of stearic acid, came from watching my sister dust off her offspring with zinc oxide powder after bathing with residue floating everywhere. Our final process was not useful for baby bottoms but quite successful in recovering silver values from vast dumps of the Prince Con in Arizona. It was even tried on the tailing dumps of the Ampara mines of Matalan, Mexico.

In early 1917, clouds of war brought another change. Nestling in the foothills high above Salt Lake was Fort Douglas, a tiny red-bricked army post from early days. One day I had a phone call from Captain French, whose long army career had included some twenty five years as Captain. "McChrystal!" he barked, "How would you like to be an Army Officer?" Surprised but intrigued, I inquired cagily as to military requirements and what one must know.

I still remember the harsh slightly disgusted tone. "From the way I read the specifications and requirements, you don't have to know a god-damn thing."

With these requirements I felt quite competent and replied affirmatively, dashed to Fort Douglas for the necessary forms, got recommendations from various sources, and in a month was sworn in as 2nd Lieutenant Infantry Reserve. I was later ordered to report for duty at First Officers Training Camp, Presidio of San Francisco.

All ideas of being a flotation expert faded. I had visions of brilliant uniforms, even a star. With my suddenly acquired military bearing, I bought a swashbuckling type of raincoat to go with my Stanford sombrero, said farewell to Salt Lake friends and relatives, then went to Eureka for a final visit.

This last week was dramatic. I strode around with what I assumed was the look of a veteran campaigner. Mother was misty-eyed; Dad looked up at me, being much shorter. I met my yearlong friends on the plank sidewalks of Main Street. There was a feature story of my successful past and unquestionably successful future, personally written by Editor-Publisher of the *Eureka Reporter.* A few items of "off-duty" clothing were selected at Shriver's Haberdashery, naturally at military discount. There were political discussions with Denis J. O'Sullivan, news pundit and owner of Eureka's most elegant saloon; and a quick dash up Church Street to see Father Donohue, dropout from Dublin High, whose weekly sermons were either "Hell" or "Damnation," with specials for Christmas and Easter. I made a nostalgic visit to the Picture Palace, recalling the piano stylings of my first love, also the unremoved white gloves.

I departed from the tiny railroad station, bound for Salt Lake, adventure and glory.

Arthur J. McChrystal

2. Ninety-Day Wonder

1917-1921

When Company 9 Officers Training Camp (O.T.C.) lined up in front of their red-brick barracks, across from the Western Department Headquarters, Presidio of San Francisco, it was evident that the members were more ambitious than military. However, I had a minute store of military knowledge, gained from high-school days, which was my left foot and the manual of arms. This gave me such a distinct advantage over the majority of trainees that I later took and passed the Examinations for Provisional Lieutenants, Regular Army, with only 1000 to be selected from all training camps. However I did discover that there were a few more things about the profession of arms.

Attitude. One of the enlisted instructors had shot himself. Comment by a thirty year sergeant: "Damn fool. Kills himself half an hour before lunch and four days before payday."

Simplicity. The problem was the construction of a complete trench system along the heights overlooking the Presidio. My portion was the construction of an underground latrine. I arranged everything but television, which was not yet in existence.

The comment of my instructor, a be-medaled French veteran: "Nevair, nevair make ze latrine in the trenches, as you make ze soldiers eat ze lunch zere."

Map making and Distance Estimation were done on the Presidio Golf Club, which I knew very well, especially the rough. In Tactics we young potential field marshals accomplished movements unheard of in modern warfare. During the maneuver between the traditional Red and Blue forces the Red right flank gave way, the center held, and the left smartly advanced giving a whirligig effect never before demonstrated in military maneuvers. Another remarkable effort was when the pet setter dog, darling of an unpopular instructor, dashed barking between the rival lines to receive a combined hail of paper bullets from blank cartridges. There were cheers and yelps as the dog disappeared and the instructional comments were far from laudatory.

There was another on *Attitude*. On the last payday before graduation, the company stood in a long line before the Paymaster's desk. As called, individuals would step forward, salute, pick up the pay, and depart. Late in the line was a professional Southerner type. When his name was called, he slouched forward to the table drawling, "Mah pay ain't wuth salutin a damn nigger." There was a dead silence, then the distinguished-looking colored major of the then Pay Corps, calmly rose, took off his coat and draped it over the chair. "If you want your money, soldier. salute those shoulder straps." The colored major was an officer and a great gentleman.

With graduation came two of my life's major events: my appointment as 2nd Lieutenant Infantry, Regular Army and my marriage to Marion Bliss, daughter of George Bliss, California and Nevada cattle baron and San Francisco resident. Marion was deeply religious, patient, and a wonderful mother. But she was not interested in my career.

My first assignment was the 22nd Machine Gun Battalion, 8th Division, Camp Fremont, located on the Stanford campus, with General Morrison commanding. As a divisional battalion we were given first choice on draft cards of men, predominantly from the northwest – timbermen and tree toppers. My first three squads averaged six-feet three, and willing to fight with teeth, boots or even guns, if necessary.

As a regular division our hopes for overseas action were high, only to gradually fall, as it was apparent that "Blackjack" Pershing didn't like "Daddy" Morrison. So we fought the Battle of Camp Fremont. As divisional machine gun instructor I had ample time to work on my favorite weapon, the '45 automatic, as well as teach my loggers to operate the British Vickers and later our own Browning machine gun. But the majority professed their preference for boots, especially for close-up work.

In September I sneaked a quick trip to Vladivostok as an ADC to General Graves, the principle feature being the near-capsizing of our transport as we passed close to a bathing beach filled with Russian belles of all sizes and shapes, sans suits.

General Graves had previously inspected our division, finding us "unready for overseas service" and was then given command. Magically we were then "fit for service."

Then another tragedy – the great flu epidemic. Standard form: 103 degrees temperature and the hospital. It was October when the division, flu-ridden, frustrated and fuming, was ordered to Long Island for embarkation. I used ice-cubes to reduce my temperature, so I wouldn't miss the trip. Embarkation Center, Long Island, was pure confusion: supplies needed and unneeded, multi-paged rosters constantly changing with ever additional copies.

There were a few illegal trips to New York and the memory of a Sunday morning hangover at the Aster, with porter Mike Mulhall advising, "Try a church, boys. They're all good and might not harm yuh."

Amid excitement and confusion the division embarked November 6 and the blacked-out transport assembled off Fire Island. On the evening of November 11, 1918, Armistice Day, we steamed slowly back to Hoboken Pier. Part of the 8th Division sailed later for occupation duty, but the thrill was gone. My battalion was ordered to Camp Lee, Virginia for demobilization and discharge.

Here I learned another adage: Don't trust anybody! My Mess Sergeant, a veteran of over thirty years' service, was on leave prior to retirement. His replacement, a young college graduate, came into the Orderly Room with a thick sheaf of papers.

"Sir!" he said, saluting sharply, "These look like unpaid company bills!" He was right – a total of over $800, from a Richmond Supply House. The company fund was less than $50.00 following special meals and entertainment. We dashed into Richmond looking for the salesman. No luck, but on his desk was a short note from my former Mess Sergeant: "Dear Pete, Charge the next case of cigarettes as a barrel of mixed pickles. Thanks, Yours, Joe."

When Sgt. Joe returned a few days later I showed him the bills and his note. He flushed, then paled, stammered something about a mistake that he would straighten out. "Don't worry about those bills, Sergeant," I said. "You have a problem and a choice. Retire next week as a Master Sergeant or get a nice long vacation at Ft. Leavenworth. If you choose retirement, I want $800.00 on my desk by 5:30 this afternoon!" The money was on my desk by the deadline and a week later he was discharged as Master Sergeant. Possibly a wrong decision, but thirty-odd years service is a long stretch.

My original starting point, Fort Douglas, Utah was my next assignment: 1st Battalion 21st Infantry, charged with the perilous duty of guarding a wire-stockade of interned German aliens, all civilians. Main duty: a twice weekly guard tour with unannounced nightly inspections.

One night I entered a spotless kitchen to hear running feet and detect a most interesting odor. On the kitchen range was a large container of spoiled apricots plus a still manufactured from flat oyster cans. As a graduate chemist, I thought the equipment deserved further attention and removed it to my quarters, where I had been doing some research work on grapefruit juice, neglecting the package instructions showing how to keep the product from becoming alcoholic. Incidentally, the tested apricot distillate tasted terrible.

Another prisoner occupation was baseball, played with a German accent. There was also gardening. The latter produced flowers, vegetables and an almost successful prison break. A tunnel, starting under a mess hall and extending some 200 feet to a clump of bushes outside the electrified wire fence, had been dug with kitchen knives and other utensils; dirt was pulled out in sacks and mixed with garden soil. Plus there was an elaborate warning system for approaching sentries.

The tunnel was large enough to permit the passage of a medium-sized body. According to later reports on an attempted breakout, the tunnel was filled with intended escapees. Three had crawled out and gained concealment, unnoticed by the night sentries. Number Four was a mistake: not only was he a trifle oversize, but he had taken with him a small case and was completely stuck near the tunnel exit. His struggles drew the attention of the wall guards, who immediately opened up with a machine gun burst. The three escapees were cornered, sirens blew, and the foot-first German retreat from the tunnel became a classic comedy.

Early in 1920 the American Olympic Rifle and Pistol trials were held at Camp Kearney, now part of the US Navy Station, Miramar, California. I was extremely fortunate in winning the pistol trials and decided to relax after weeks of training. Just across the border was Tijuana, with a racetrack, numberless bars and a casino. Wearing some rather oversized civilian clothes, borrowed from Archie Schreve, a prominent San Diego lawyer, and with a young air corps officer, I went across the border. Between bad judgment and "boiler makers," our funds almost disappeared. But on the last race we hit a 40 to 1 shot. When the local police started pushing us towards the pay-off windows, planning to get it back at the Casino, we decided an honorable thing was to slug a couple. Winnings collected, we fought a rear guard action to the Casino ... run ... stop ... slug ... and run.

Once safely inside, we encountered a really select group: "Fatty" Arbuckle, who had had some recent rape trouble at the St. Francis Hotel; Norman Selby, former Kid McCoy, champion boxer, who had taken a course at a California pen for wife mistreatment; plus a few others. The return border-crossing was vague; so was a crap game in some apartment. I noticed that Mr. McCoy was skidding his dice and not bouncing them against the wall, told him he was a crooked so-and-so, and asked him to make something out of it. Fortunately, on-lookers interfered.

For many years afterwards when I would be sitting in judgment on some hapless soldier, I would think of the aggregate penalty I could have received for being across the border in war-time – drunk and very disorderly, slugging officials of a friendly nation, and illegal gambling. Plus I could have been in Leavenworth for years. My later judgments tempered accordingly.

With the resumption of Allied Games in Brussels in 1920, track became my special interest, regimental meets, department meets ... the Army Final at Boston. I did fairly well there, but at the Allied Games my broad jumping was not quite broad enough.

Following the Allied Games I was ordered to Western Department Headquarters at the Presidio, and was given extra duty as Assistant Education and Recreation Officer. This last was a vaguely conceived program using millions of surplus non-appropriated funds, making Phi Beta Kappas out of soldiers with mathematical experience largely gained by reading spots on dice. We finally made it semi-practicable: plumbing for Post plumbers, cooking for Company cooks, electrical operations for Post electricians. It took nearly a year for this monstrosity to disappear, together with available funds.

In 1921, then a Captain and slightly beset with mother-in-laws on both sides, my then small family and myself were delighted when orders were received to report for duty with Headquarters, U. S. Forces, Tientsin, China.

My only sadness during the period was the loss of my father during the flu epidemic.

3. Nine and Out!

My two years at the Infantry School with the 29th Infantry (Instructional Regiment) were not particularly eventful but were far from dull. Fort Benning in 1925 was not the elaborate and complicated set-up of today. Housing was simple – rows of long wooden shacks for soldiers and two-story wooden apartment buildings for officers, faculty, as well as students.

A week after we moved into our quarters, a backing-up coal delivery truck moved quietly into our living room, coal and all, when the driver's brakes failed. Fortunately domestic servants were plentiful, even if slightly burr-headed and untrained. A remarkable example of crossing a language barrier was the ability of a colored maid and our Chinese nurse to sit and chat fluently for hours, with neither one understanding a word.

Shortly after my arrival I was made a member of the squad trying out for the Camp Perry Matches, specializing in my favorite weapon, the pistol. I was on the firing range when an orderly arrived with word that I was wanted at Post Headquarters.

It didn't take long. When I reported to Brig. General Briant Wells, Commandant, he informed me that General Court Martial Charges against me had been received from Headquarters US Forces China. Breathtaking, but the details even more so. I was accused under Articles of War of conspiring with two noncommissioned officers to defraud the government by permitting them to draw pay and allowances while they were disabled with venereal disease … further, that I had concealed the fact of their suffering from venereal disease in order to better my military efficiency record. These charges – four in all, preferred by my good friend, Brigadier General William D. Connor! When asked by General Wells just what had happened, I told him frankly what had been done by myself and other company commanders to protect old-time non-coms from results of the situation in China, regardless of command orders. I further told him that War Department records would show that I did not need to further my efficiency records. Finally, I told him of the General Connor and Mrs. Connor incident. For the first time, there was a slight smile on the Commandant's face.

"Captain McChrystal," he remarked, slowly, "I don't think that you displayed the best judgment, but on the other hand, I know the situation in the Orient. I am returning the charges to China with a recommendation that the entire matter be dropped. Now go to work on your shooting instead of conversation."

I was a very shaky pistol-shot when I got back on the range, and even more shaky when I later discovered that the particular Article of War as charged involved mandatory dismissal from the service if found guilty!

It was nearly two months before the next news came – two months of worry and wondering. Then came the word from the War Department that the recommendation of General Wells had been disregarded and that, at the personal request of General Connor to Chief of Staff, Lt. Col. Marshall, was that an example should be made of me. I would be brought to trial. In the meantime my wife and family had returned to San Francisco for a visit, thinking everything was in order.

From then on it was a fight! My defense lawyer found out about Connors' request on the War Department. Through the AGO I secured copies of all efficiency reports since my entry into the service – all Superior, except one that contained the statement, "Officer lacks experience." This was when I had less than two years service! To further fight, I secured the services of one of the most respected lawyers in Columbus, Georgia. In the meantime I had received sworn affidavits from the two non-coms concerned to the effect that at no time had they suffered from venereal disease – affidavits accompanied by medical reports from military doctors and civilian doctors in Tientsin. I was never put under arrest in any way but it was hard not to worry, especially with a life career at stake.

My trial was probably one of the shortest General Courts Martial on record. At the conclusion of the evidence for the prosecution, my attorneys made a motion that the case be dropped. The members of the court, all senior officers, agreed in open court.

Frankly, I took a great deal of pleasure in sending Brigadier General Connor a special delivery letter, enclosing an official copy of the trial records, with the expressed hope that he would be pleased with the result. I also added my best regards to Madame Connor. Funny, I never did get a reply.

The trial knocked any chances for that year's team, either rifle or pistol, but everything was much more pleasant from that time onwards. Besides pistol-shooting my company had charge of "Scouting and Patrolling" – a "Cops and Robbers cum Daniel Boone" operation. This was never particularly enjoyed by officer students, particularly one requirement calling on the class to crawl under and through barbed-wire entanglements with the proper "tail-down" position, being assisted occasionally by low overhead machine gun fire. Armor was beginning to get full attention under the then-Major "Shrimp" Milburn with the first organized tank battalion alternately cruising around and breaking down. Night operations were looked on with favor, as tactics learned could be applied to evening journeys to "Preston's Farm," a nearby but forbidden source of prohibited "corn."

Information of various kinds gained as an Instructor was helpful when I finally took the Company Officers' Course. It was in these two years that I was in close contact with a large number of future greats: Bedell Smith, John Dahlquist, Ted Wessels, Charlie Bolte, Joe Collins and Lawton Collins, among many others.

Upon graduation, I was ordered to Georgia Tech in Atlanta where, as Assistant Professor of Military Science and Tactics, my main job was coaching freshmen ends and place kickers for Coach Bill Alexander, coaching a city league team of ex-college basketball players, whose idea of training was never to drink corn whiskey unless it was at least a month old.

One assignment was the protocol and placement of units in the annual Confederate Memorial Day Parade. As the first Northerner selected for the job, I used a simple alphabetical system. I had the "Amalgamated Daughters of the Confederacy" placed ahead of the "Sons and Daughters of This and That," who should have been five places behind ... plus many other violations of established tradition. Ensuing protests to my Chief, Colonel Earl D'Arcy Pearce, himself an old Atlantean, insured that there would never be another Northerner on the job.

Feeling young and gay, and certainly in excellent condition, I tried another change. At the suggestion of Captain "Buzz" Glen, later to be a 3-star Air Corps general, I took flying lessons, passed the physical at Maxwell Field and forwarded my application for transfer from Infantry to the then "Aviation Section of the US Signal Corps." Having been a golfing partner of "Hap" Arnold at the Presidio in the days when he was being chastised for backing Billy Mitchell's bombers, I sent the application direct to him in Washington. It took four days to get a reply – a brief private letter. "What in hell do you think an old fossil like yourself could do in the Aviation Section? Regards, Hap"

He later smoothed my injured feelings by inviting me to Washington to see one of the first "talking pictures" ... a little De Forrest "squawk" box with pictures ... shown to the War Department as something possibly useful for training pictures.

My supposed promotional, athletic, and public relations ability was probably responsible for my transfer from Georgia Tech to Ft.

Thomas, Kentucky. Prior to reporting, I departed on a visit to my favorite home town San Francisco, leaving instructions for packing and shipping my household goods. There was apparently a slight error in that I received a telegram from the packer that "Your box of professional books is leaking." This was corrected by transferring title to a couple of thirsty naval colleagues remaining at Tech.

Fort Thomas, a tiny, handkerchief-sized post, perched high on the Ohio River banks, was originally built to protect Cincinnati from possible attacks by Confederate gunboats, in the event they could get up stream. This never happened and as a military post, Ft. Thomas continued to provide good government spending for the local merchants as well as serving as a respectable neighborhood for nearby Covington, Kentucky – the recognized "rest and recreational" area for tired gangsters from Cincinnati across the river.

This was one of the "poverty" periods of the Army, with every nickel counted, with resultant "do-it-yourself" activities on army posts. Professional boxing had been barred for several years in Ohio but was legal in Kentucky, and Ft. Thomas was only a dime car-ride away. An agile-minded Post Commander, Colonel Waldron, decided to stage professional boxing bouts on the post, the participants being alleged members of the Army Reserve. From the start the idea was a winner – every Thursday night crowds of fight-hungry fans would assemble in the Post gym, and the proceeds made a welcome addition to the local Post Fund. Then Ohio voters decided boxing could be legalized and Ft. Thomas bouts lost their monopoly. And the weekly take dropped from thousands to a few hundred.

It was shortly after this when I reported to my new Commanding Officer, Colonel Wm. H. Waldron, 10th Infantry. He definitely informed me that my military knowledge was not required – my job was to get the fights going again and start the money coming in. For almost two years I was the Company Commander of A Company, 10th Infantry, with an actual muster strength of one husky Irish First

Sergeant, who served as my private secretary and bodyguard when arguments got rough, plus three company clerks taking care of ticket sales, book-keeping, and doubling as ticket sellers.

I arranged with the Colonel that I would report to him directly and not to his staff. A special stipulation, due to existent prohibition laws, he was not to examine too closely expenditures "entertainment and refreshments for newspaper writers."

First move was to stop the bouts for three weeks, in the meantime getting the hall in shape – additional front row seats and raised gallery seats in the back.

That afternoon I was sitting in the office of Joe Nolan, *Cincinnati Enquirer,* Dean of sportswriters, who became my mentor, advisor and friend. Joe taught me commercial sportswriting technique of writing the same material four different ways to match four different papers.

Through Nolan I met two unusual characters, unusual in that they were honest. There are no longer many honest men in the professional boxing ranks. These honest men were Danny Davis, an honest manager and Lou Bauman, an honest referee. Davis had an excellent stable of young fighters, including a left-hander, Freddy Miller, a featherweight, later to become world's champion.

The Grand Opening Night was terrific. The 10th Infantry Indoor Polo team had played indoors during the winter season with the famed Camargo Hunt Team – the Harrison Smiths, Paul Crossleys, Vanderbilts, fellow polo players and now fellow boxing patrons. The front row filled with polo-playing elite, press and politicians, radio time, at bargain prices. The headliner was Freddy Miller of Cincinnati, future champion, with four-way press stories written by Joe Nolan and myself, alternately. It was a great evening, well over five thousand. The Colonel did remark that the consumption of such quantities of raspberry soda and coca-cola by sport writers could be harmful, but he permitted me to be responsible for their health as long as the fight write-ups were good.

It was through Joe Nolan and Referee Lou Bauman, plus some head work, that the operation move steadily upward. By the time Freddy Miller had won the featherweight championship, the weekly take was running around fifteen thousand, and the accomplishments of Company A 10th Infantry were well thought of. One glaring exception was occasioned by a rather peculiar assignment policy. Company A 10th Infantry echelon consisted of myself, two lieutenants, one first sergeant and four company clerks, all connected directly with the fight operations. As for the balance of the personnel, I never saw them. On paper there were only soldiers of the regiment absent without leave, sick in hospital with VD, who were usually transferred to the roster of Company A. Frankly, if the War Department or my old friend of the China days, General Connor, had ever closely examined the record-breaking misdeed accomplishments I would have been awarded some kind of a medal. But that didn't happen and the money continued to pour in. So everybody was happy.

There was even a social aspect to the fight program, besides the regular attendance of the polo set. One evening a sudden cloudburst forced the cancellation of the fight program, featuring a coming welter that I had secured on a good percentage but only minimal guarantee. With the idea of getting a future bout at equally advantageous prices I invited the fighter, his manager, his very buxom bride, Lou Baurnan, the referee and several sport writers to my quarters to partake of a few goblets of raspberry soda. The evening was very successful until Referee Bauman demonstrated how a fighter breaks from a clinch by rocking, breaking the rhythm, and slapping the freed glove on the opponent's chin. I was assisting in the demonstration when Lou's swing came a little inside and failed to clear my chin. After a long count, I was reclining on the over-stuffed lap of the fighter's bride, inhaling a modified version of Chanel #5. Ammonia would have been preferable. Later in the evening I was permitted a glimpse into processes of the female mind.

The name of Johnny Datto, a promising lightweight, had been mentioned, and the bride looked up with sudden interest. "You know, Cap, dat guy tried to make me in a dance hall in Toledo one night."

In properly shocked tones, I remarked, "No? Really?" And then, "What did you do?" "Natch, Cap, I repulsed his advances. But he persisted. And I tells him he ain't had no proper interduction, and I was there with another gent. But," she continued with a reminiscent smile, "he kept on botherin' me."

I played straight man. "He did? And what did you do?" "Well, Cap," she sighed in pleasant memory, "When the dance was over, I goes out with my gent friend and I sees the guy crossing the street. And then, Oh Boy, Ah hauls off and hits him square in the ass with me Chrysler roadster!"

With a Ford or Chevy, the woman's honor would not have been satisfied, but a Chrysler!

It was my steadily growing local fame as a boxing promoter that got me into a venture on my own. One night the bouts were over and, together with my small staff, we were enjoying some excellent special raspberry soda when two well-dressed fans entered the office and announced themselves as members of the American Legion from Apalachicola, West Virginia. Frankly, I was not impressed until they mentioned that the local coal mining company was planning on holding a boxing card on the Fourth of July for the first time in the history of the town. In the course of the conversation I suggested the type of card they should have – a main event ten, a semi-final six and the remainder of the bill to be filled out with local boy four-rounders ... and wished them good luck. To my surprise I received a telegram stating that everything was arranged and to go ahead and book the bouts. As we were playing polo in Cleveland on July 3rd, the timing was bad but I wired back asking just how much they were getting from the coal company. The answering information, "Five Thousand," inspired my Scottish ancestry self and I started to work, confirming the date.

As this was to be their first professional fight program it was better to start at the bottom of the ladder, or near it. My good friend, Manager Danny Davis, had a stableful of young hopefuls who could be depended upon to put up a first-class scrap, especially as they all trained together. A short telephone call to Danny, and the entire program was fixed up. My dependable featherweight, Freddy Miller, then on his way to a world's championship, versus a stalemate as the main event … a couple of slow heavyweights thoroughly versed in each other's style, if any, as the semi-final six-rounder. Danny was to load all four and himself into a car and report to me on the morning of July Fourth at the best, if only, hotel in Apalachicola. Everything was set, even the payment – an even split of the fire. A wire was sent to my clients informing them that they could expect a great main event program, brimful of action, following up with expert write-ups regarding the various fighters, authentic in that I wrote them myself. Not knowing the names of Freddie's opponent and the participants in the semi-final, I assigned them appropriate Irish and Italian titles, definitely not contained in official ring annals. Later discovery that one was a Swede and the other two colored boys was passed up as immaterial.

With everything arranged, I departed peacefully with the 10th Infantry Polo team for a match in Cleveland. With the finish of the Sunday afternoon match I didn't even change from sweaty polo clothes but jumped into the car and headed for Ft. Thomas, stopping just long enough to change and pick up a suitcase and some restoratives. Then southward through Kentucky via Cumberland Gap, to my destination – grimy, dirty, coal-dusted Apalachicola, West Virginia. After an all night drive arrived, with eyes barely open, I located the hotel where Danny and entourage were waiting. Handbills and posters were everywhere, quoting generously from the write-ups I had furnished … "OPERA HOUSE … 8 p.m." "Admission Free"

My next stop was at the Opera House to check on arrangements. Outside of large posters and handbills there was nothing. Danny and I finally dug out the aged caretaker, introduced ourselves and inquired about essentials – the ring, ring mat, plus other items.

"Hell, you all is the promoter, ain't yuh?" he drawled, as he leaned back and spat accurately at a small knothole. "Don't you all bring the ring and them things?"

When I explained that such articles were usually furnished and that my car didn't have the carrying capacity of a truck, he slowly rose and took another difficult angle shot at the knothole. "Come on fellers, lets git over to the store."

The store was open but empty. Everyone was at the Grand Parade. From stock we cut enough inch rope to make a rough twenty foot square with two strands, some two-by-fours for ring posts, an old tarp for the ring mat, a hammer and some nails. In a dusty corner we found some old angle iron to serve as a bell. The entire group, fighters and all, returned to the Opera House. We rigged up a rough ring with two front posts along the lamp-lit footlights and the back post supported by clothesline tied to some old scenery, probably from "Uncle Tom's Cabin." With the unpadded tarp laid in place, securely tacked down, angle irons hung in the corner, everything was ready for the evening's production.

Everything was ready, but I hadn't contacted the committee with the view of getting a heavy advance on the promised five thousand. In the fight game, money has its virtues and its problems. I had instructed Danny and the fighters to go to the hotel, eat and meet me at the arena at 7:30. I also went to the hotel with the idea of getting a little sleep. My room was reminiscent of the Black Hole of Calcutta, in that every window was thoroughly coal-dusted and opaque. Dropping down on one of the three cots I fell into a dreamless slumber, occasionally interrupted by a biting sensation.

By evening the town was really organized. The drum corps battles had been a great success and the hour-long parade had left onlookers with a monstrous thirst, which was apparently being well satisfied.

I had changed into my "promoter's" number, a brown suit and red tie, and had managed a few bites from a cindered steak, reposing on watery "mashed and gravy," plus a few slugs of local moonshine, presented by admirers, seeing for the first time a renowned promoter from the Big Leagues. Everything was fine, except for the money. At about seven I arrived at the Opera House, already jammed to the rafters. I checked Danny and his boys in the "Stars Dressing Room" and was escorted to a place of honor at the ringside, with two vacant seats adjoining, for the absent committeemen.

The four-round prelims were more remarkable for willingness than boxing skill, but, with the help of more home-brew, put the audience into the proper mood. But with no committeemen, money worry started settling in like a Los Angeles fog.

There was an intermission following the two preliminaries.

I crawled through the ropes as the angle-iron bell clanged, very natty with my blue shirt and red armbands – the later the mark of a high-class referee. After some applause I proceeded to announce the officials – Danny Davis as Timekeeper, myself as Referee, and gave the name of two locals, drafted as seconds.

As the two husky semi-finalists entered the ring, one of them tripped over the lower rope, causing the entire structure to collapse. This was quickly rectified with some spare clothes-line, then came the introductions. Here I realized my pre-fight publicity was not exactly accurate – Fighting Mike Clancy was a round-faced blond Swede and Battling Antonio, a definitely Deep South product. Regardless, the six rounds were good and reasonably fast.

The boys had worked together so long in the gym that every move was routine – terrific punches spatting on going-away shoulders, whistling uppercuts barely missing. The bout would have been a wonder on television, but, alas, a few years too soon. When I lifted both hands for a well-earned and well-played draw, cheers resounded through the house.

Then the main event – Champion Freddy Miller of Cincinnati and
Ft. Thomas versus Slashing Sammy Somebody (the name forgotten).
Ten rounds ... ten ... to a decision. Meantime I could see that the
seats of our committeemen were still vacant.

To stall further, we went into several details about the bout, tossed a
couple pairs of well-worn and knuckle-broken gloves into the audience to further convey the idea the coming event would be practically a bare fist slug fest, worthy of the days of old John L. Sullivan.
Readjusting my red arm bands,

I called the boys together for fight instructions, under the simple ring
lighting of clusters of fifty watt lamps. As the house lights dimmed
I added a few quiet and practical words: "Listen, boys, there may be
some kind of a slipup – the guys that promised the dough haven't
shown up yet – so a sudden knock-out might leave us holding an
empty sack." ... "AND COME OUT FIGHTING!"

The clang of the angle-iron – Round one! Southpaw Freddy sprang
from his corner – deftly touched gloves – and swung into a vicious
attack against the well-muscled ribs of the Slasher. Slasher backed
away, then retaliated with a series of smashing right and left hooks
to the Miller chin. That is, they would have hit the Miller chin if the
Miller glove hadn't interposed. The crowd jumped to its feet as the
champ in turn backed away, to resume the attack with a whistling left
that just grazed the Slasher chin. A right jab, then a hay-maker left.
Stumbling slightly on the loose canvas, Freddy's aim was a trifle off.
Instead of grazing, the left landed flush on the Slasher bottom. Down
he went, flat and limp, with only a minute ten seconds of Round One,
and no committee men with the money.

"One ... two ... three" (*sotto voce,* "Get up, you bum.") "four ... Get
back to your corner, Miller ... back ... back ... five ..." The Slasher
stirred. "... six ..." The Slasher was on his knees. "... seven ... eight
..." and he was up, as Miller moved in for the kill, or a reasonable

imitation. The Slasher clinched, with Miller holding him upright with a right hand held firmly under the Slasher's arm-pits … then the clang of the angle iron.

Timekeeper Danny had noticed the continued absence of the money men and had cut nearly a minute off the round. I walked over to the Slasher corner where the second was working on him and could see his eyes were beginning to focus. This was a temporary relief. The next two rounds were terrific, or seemed so. The Slasher, coming back, rocked the advancing Miller with a wild right. The champion had apparently lost his timing and his swings were missing, at least they were missing until I heard a muttered "I'm OK" from the Slasher.

In the pause between the third and fourth rounds there was a slight commotion in the hall, and down towards the ringside came several belated arrivals. Apparently there had been a heated argument over the election of a new American Legion Commander and the entire Committee, including my two finance boys, had been delayed. The group seated themselves as Danny clanged for the next round. Freddy, the Champ, was being out-pointed and out-slugged by the Slasher. The worried look on his face deserved a fistic Oscar.

There was a roar of applause as the group filled up the vacant front row seats, and the greatest, a hail from my two boys, "Hi there, Cap! It's great show!"

At the end of the round the sagging ropes allowed me to bend and confidentially remark that my fighters would be leaving immediately after the fights ... and about the guarantee. A quick fumble in a hip pocket and out came a sheaf of green etchings bearing the likeness of Benjamin Franklin. Danny delayed the start of Round Six for a few seconds, but it doesn't take long to count fifty hundreds. I tucked the wadded notes into my hip pocket and, as the boys came together I remarked to Freddy, "We've got the dough."

Suddenly the tide of battle changed again. Back-pedaling, Freddy the Champ surged forward, right hand poised, then a lightening left, this time flush to the Slasher's chin. "One … two …" Miller moved to his corner. "…three …" Slasher still motionless. "… eight … nine … and OUT!" There was a shocked silence, then the crowd realized that Freddy the Champion had come through for good old Apalachicola!

Arm in arm, Freddy and the Slasher departed for the dressing room. As becomes a promoter, I leaned nonchalantly against the wobbly ring post, receiving plaudits for "the greatest fight ever seen in Apalachicola." It was a good one at that.

Even my tired feelings were gone with the "after the show mood," helped by a few slugs of Virginia's best untaxed health restorer. There was an elaborate banquet at the Apalachicola equivalent of the Ritz – the same stringy steak with mashed and gravy, the Official Ball with couples whirling in a terpsichorean traffic jam, the crowning of Queen Carbon – a dream in an almost white tule dress, offers to conduct another bout... Sure, but next month, next year. By now all I wanted was sleep.

Upstairs in the Black Hole replica, another customer had taken the cot by the window. Regardless, I stripped off my clothes and flung myself on the remaining bed. Sleep, sweet sleep, sound and undisturbed … until I felt the vague restless feeling I'd had during my afternoon nap. Here it was again. The light of a dim lamp globe revealed the cause of my unrest: my wondering about the grayish-white sheets. Stifling a moan and hoping my aching head would not explode, I painfully dressed, made my way downstairs past a sleeping porter, slid into my car and headed north, away from Apalachicola … and fights.

4. Old China Hand

1921-25

In 1921 the westward wallow of the old U.S. Army Transport "Thomas" was no luxury cruise. While refrigerator facilities were sufficient to carry food for round trip … San Francisco to Manila and return … air conditioning was unknown, and with a speed of a crawling eight to nine knots with stops at Honolulu and Guam, the voyage was a long tiresome twenty-eight days. Jammed with young officer couples plus progeny … I had two myself … the initial fear that one or more of the many infants would fall overboard changed gradually to a hope that certain ones would. Regulation required woolen, high-necked uniforms became scratchy when we hit the tropics … chit-chat and bridge comments became even more so as we sailed along.

Besides the daily ship pool bringing comments like, "Is this damn tub backing up?" the principal event was the almost obligatory daily bath. Old George, gray-haired colored bath steward, ignored possible embarrassment or card game involvement. "Missy, you alls bath is done ready. You done missed for three days!" He steadfastly refused furlough, claiming, "Suh! One time I wuz gone on furlough and when I got back them baths jest wasn't fit fur quality folk!"

George, around fifty in those days, is now probably running a celestial bathhouse.

Leaving tropical Guam, passengers rejoiced at sighting the green shoreline of the Philippines. Itchy collars were again hooked up, children recounted, and hand baggage hastily assembled. Past the menacing, supposedly impregnable fortress of Corregidor was the welcome sight of the Manila docks. High ceilinged and fan-cooled rooms of the Manilla Hotel were heaven-like after month-long stuffiness of a transport cabin, even if lizard-like "geccos" on the ceiling could drop at any minute. Native tailors feverishly stitched white and khaki uniforms, ready in twenty-four hours and looking like it. Male and female arrivals crowded the long hotel bar, welcome after four weeks of regulation-enforced prohibition.

Two days later we sailed to Tangku on the China Sea, the nearest port to Tientsin, this time on a smaller but equally slow transport. First land sighted was the sheer cliffs and green mountains of Formosa, with sparkling rivulets plunging boldly into the sea. This tiny paradise later became Taiwan, home base for Nationalist Chinese and aged Marshal Chiang Kai Shek. In eight days we landed, our sea voyage ended.

From the ship we were loaded onto the so-called "Allied Train," a military train, operated jointly by the then occupying powers with a specific mission, dating from the Boxer Days, of "keeping the line open from Peking to the sea. From the look of the equipment I thought we would be lucky to make Tientsin. At the sprawling Tientsin Station confusion upon confusion … shouting baggage coolies fighting over possession of hand luggage, battles broken up by native police with efficient and heavy clubs, greetings by army friends and others, filth everywhere … complete chaos. But husky non-coms with a few Chinese commands, plus an occasional well-placed boot, aided by anxious owners, gradually sorted out luggage-and individuals. New arrivals, children, luggage and all were placed in rickshaws and the cavalcade started at a brisk trot towards previously assigned quarters. Except for a few diplomatic automobiles and trucks, motor transport was then unknown.

Our quarters … future home for the ensuing four years … was a two-story brick house, "Villa Jeanne D'Arc," blocks away from the main officers' quarters on Race Course Road, but close to the .American Headquarters and troop barracks.

As we entered our compound gate, I was greeted by a smiling faced and bowing group, headed by a tall figure in a flowing white robe.

"You velly welcome, Master. Me Number One Boy. These are you servant ... they work you!"

"My God!" I inquired from the officer accompanying us, "How can I pay nine servants, particularly if they work me?"

Meantime, the Number One Boy had supervised the unloading and stowing away of baggage, brought up a tray of drinks plus dainty cakes. And two "amahs" had already started spoiling our two infants.

"Don't worry! I think that you can make it. The nine will cost you altogether around twenty dollars a month, and they feed themselves! However, you'll need a private rickshaw boy ... and that will be another three dollars."

Relieved, with the children taken over and enamored by non-English speaking nurses, we departed for the Tientsin Club to start an almost carefree four years as an Old China Hand. My first drink – Black Label Scotch and soda, costing approximately eight cents. Later this rose to twelve cents, which almost caused a revolution among the older club members.

Would you have liked nine household servants, costing fifteen dollars a month and no overtime? No automobile, but hand-driven rickshaws, costing another three dollars a month ... slow, but economic transport. A variety of sports ... football, baseball, horse racing, golf and even elbow lifting. The last named sport was very popular, with the prices right. Gordon Gin: fifty cents a fifth ... Red Label, seventy ... Black Label at ninety ... and whiskey soda at a luxurious English club a dime a drink. The local dynamite distilled from gaoliang roots ran a mere two cents per drink, but the taste was quite off-beat.

This was Tientsin, China, in the middle 'twenties and the old China hands included the 15th U.S. Infantry, China, some 700 strong.

Cheap and easy living with only normal garrison duties and a special two months a year "hunting leave" if requested ... a combination of mild espionage and excellent hunting in areas ranging from Manchuria to Tibet.

Occupation of various Chinese cities and ports, including Tientsin, Peking and Tsingtao, by foreign troops was the direct result of the Boxer Rebellion of 1900, continued with the fall of the Empress Dowager in 1911. Initially the occupying forces included English, French, Russian, Japanese, German, Italian, and American troops, with a token representation by Austria. In Tientsin, with the exception of the Americans, occupying forces took over and held specific areas outside the native portion of the city. The Americans, as usual, paid for their holdings but the price wasn't too high. With the end of WWI concessions of the Russians, Germans, and Austrians were given up and the Italian contingent was a token and obsolete naval force. "Kaiser Wilhelm Strasse" became an extension of "Victoria Road," and an enormous old Chinese cemetery in the Russian zone, across the Pei Ho River, became the Tientsin Golf Club.

Military duty was not too severe – usual inspections, close order drill, and occasional field exercises, often going as far as two or three miles from the city, preparing the troops for instant action in case of a war that wasn't and couldn't be. The main emphasis was on physical training and outdoor sports with the objective of taking the troops' mind off other indoor sports, very popular in China and in many other places in the world.

This problem of troops stationed for long periods in a foreign land is one going back to the days of the Crusaders. It was V.D., not the Romans, that delayed Hannibal in his march on Rome.

During my China days the situation was basic. The pay of a. lowly private at that time was $36.00 per month. Exchanged into "Max Dollars" at a tenfold increase in purchasing power made him a potential heavy spender. Liquor prices ranged from around ninety cents per fifth for Black Label, Gordon Gin at four bits to a good-sized slug of "Sanshu," a local dynamite distilled from gaoliang roots, available around two cents per drink. This made drinking a pleasant, inexpensive habit for the away-from-home trooper. With female companionship of homeland practically non-existent, lonesome soldiers would start looking over local products, available at prices ranging from twenty cents to two dollars for newly arrived White Russian refugees. They were all interesting, especially along clinical lines associated with their profession.

Early in my China tour a practical minded force commander set all so-called "ladies retail establishments" off-limits except for two larger places, where both inmates and customers were physically inspected before and afterwards.

The worrisome venereal rate dropped sharply during the ensuing months. Then came an imperative order from the War Department to discontinue, probably urged by a pious, impotent congressman. "Our flag will never be permitted to wave over a whorehouse!" The imaginary flag went down ... the venereal rate went up.

But enough of dull sex. A vital factor was housekeeping.

Following military procedure, I made a personal inspection of the kitchen, situated deep in the basement, which also provided living quarters for the chief cook, his assistants and several relatives, with very primitive sanitary accommodations. After a brief survey, I decided that further inspections would be unnecessarily disturbing and started to follow the magic but efficient formula for keeping healthy in China: plenty of exercise, a fair amount of liquor, occasional large doses of castor oil, and confidence!

Food itself was usually superb, if mysterious. Duck and other wild fowl were plentiful for a few cents a bird. The only danger was picking out an occasional nail or piece of rock, as market hunters would use a long-barreled gun loaded with shot, old iron and rocks crammed down on a black powder charge. With the gun, usually two barrels tied to the boat gunwale, they would slip through the tules to a flock of ducks on the water, touch off the charge with a punk stick, then pick up thirty to forty birds. Wild fowl were also netted. Fish, both salt water and fresh water, were plentiful but required constant supervision by the Number One Boy to insure freshness. Chickens, raised naturally on grain feed, were small but excellent, also most inexpensive. There were fruits of all kinds, including nuts. Pork was usually young and tender. Beef was old, stringy, and tough. Mushrooms, grown everywhere, were wonderful. Plus there were all types of vegetables.

The preparation was baffling. For instance, we had a series of fruit flavored sherbets and found one day an uncolored and rather tasteless concoction on the table. When "Number One" was queried as to just what flavor it represented, he smilingly and proudly announced, "Master, that plain flavor sherbet!"

The Number One Boy, head of the household crew, court of first and last resort, household purchasing agent, not only insured that the "cumshaw" or "squeeze" by the local: merchants did not get too far out of line, but also made it clear to all peddlers visiting the house that he, the Number One, got his regular percentage. Otherwise, "Master (or Missy) no home!"

Traditionally Number One was the only member of the staff, except the children's amah, who was spoken to in any way except for greetings. Unsatisfactory cooks or house coolies were summarily fired without special reference to Master, and a complete new crew secured immediately. With practically no telephones, except official ones, communications were usually notes carried by the rickshaw boy. This was convenient, especially in connection with social invitations. A short study of the rickshaw boy's book would show who was invited, making it possible to choose.

Another function of the various Number One Boys was connected with the spontaneous dinners organized at the Tientsin Club or bar.

An unsuspecting young hostess would suddenly discover that some twenty guests had been invited for dinner by a generous husband. No problem! The Number One Boys concerned would get together in some mysterious way, pooling current dinner resources, and in many cases, contributing needed items of china or silverware ... and occasionally placing themselves, at the disposal of the entertaining party. Parties were fun, and parties made "face" for the giver, which was essential.

A memorable incident of bachelor living: My wife and the two children, complete with mother-in-law, had returned to the States for a short visit. Rather than run a household, I kept my boy and moved in with a small group of bachelor officers. Despite our quiet way of life ... and the low cost of alcoholic beverages ... we decided that thievery must be going on in the booze department. A clever plan ... a bottle of scotch, nearly emptied, was refilled with ... well, it could have been partially scotch. A small mark was made, showing the level. We watched carefully ... the first day ... nothing. A couple of days later ... a small lowering of the level. Then a week later, almost all gone! Time for corrective action! Number One was called in.

"Look here boy! Who's been stealing our liquor?" pointing to the nearly empty bottle. "We marked the level over a week ago – practically full – and now practically empty!"

From the Number One Boy came at first a cry of protest: "Dungia... Master! Me no drink! Me White Ribbon. Sei Lee! No drinkee, no smokee." Then came a look of understanding, relief, and, possibly, of quiet amusement. "Master, that bottle, me no drink! Cook boy, he use that bottle ... put in soup!"

It was years before I could again enjoy consommé!

With today's efforts to make military life so comfortable and enjoyable for the soldier that he simply can't afford to miss the opportunity to enlist – even with the vague possibility that, he or she might have to do a little fighting – few remember the old days of foreign service when things were not too rough for even the private soldier. Over the years in China a custom had developed whereby arduous military duties such as kitchen police, sweeping barracks, washing windows, making beds and cleaning weapons and equipment were done by Chinese coolies, paid by a voluntary contribution of twenty-five cents per month. This left the troops free for other military and non-military occupations. It was an inspiring sight to see an old non-com being deftly assisted into his spotless and well-creased military jacket by his personal valet, picking up his shining coolie-cleaned rifle, then moving majestically to his place in ranks.

It was the refusal of a newly arrived soldier to pay this voluntary contribution that gave me the unenviable job of defending a murderer. This was also in the days when murder and similar criminal actions were taken seriously and not considered as a contest between justice and long-haired radical exhibitionist lawyers.

The particular soldier in question had arrived in China while his company was on the target range at Shanikwan, where the Great Wall runs into the sea. When informed as to the recognized system of payment, he flatly announced his opposition, and so was told that his failure to voluntarily contribute would result in his being placed on "kitchen police" duty under a roster system. He made his first legal mistake – a, remark: "If I do, they'll pack a damn Chinaman out of there!"

Company orders for the day detailed him on kitchen police the following morning. It was five a.m. He was seated in the screened kitchen shack quietly peeling potatoes ... with his loaded service rifle alongside him. When a Chinese coolie, collecting garbage, came to the door, the soldier picked up his rifle, shot once, then moving closer, shot him a second time through the head, then quietly resumed peeling potatoes.

As occupying force commanders were authorized to try soldier offenders for offenses against other nationals, with a first degree murder charge, I was detailed to defend. The only possible defense: "Temporary insanity!" I used every legal trick now common to today's defenders, except one. No one worried about a Chinaman, so the overworked racial angle was not used. My client was apparently moody ... heard strange noises in the night ... conflicting emotions of a stranger in a foreign land ... strained home conditions as a child of a broken home ... mutterings overheard by comrades ... the whole bag of tricks. Unfortunately, at the time, per the Manual of Courts Martial provided in the case of insanity pleas, the proceedings would he halted pending psychiatric examination. This was long before the days of the popular analyst's couch, and our medical officers were better equipped to give out pills than to rule on psycho-deficiencies. The insanity plea was rejected, leaving me only cheap legal tricks, possibly leading to a mistrial. The actual, proceedings lasted three days. One chance was that a member of the Chinese government, present throughout the trial, might interfere. But sudden queries as to his opinion, requests for his questions, were met with only an inscrutable bland smile and a headshake.

I remember the final day. The General Court had adjourned to seek a verdict. Then came a request for evidence of previous convictions, a sign that the verdict was guilty. Previous convictions, if any, and there were none, could affect the sentence. When the Court reappeared, the senior member directed both prisoner and counsel to rise. As we rose, I was shaking, and whispered, "Don't weaken." He muttered back, "I never weaken, Kid!" and stood impassively as the sentence of "confinement at hard labor for the rest of your natural life" was read.

With its hundreds of millions, life and death is still relatively unimportant in China. In the older days, before improvement of communications and transport, hundreds of thousands would die from flood, pestilence, and even hunger. Famine in one major area would find bumper crops in another. Under an old tradition, to save a life represented cheating the gods of the victim's soul, making the rescuer liable for future care of the rescued, unless the lifesaver was a member of the same family or tribe.

Coolies, unloading vessels along the Pei Ho docks, would slip and fall into the muddy waters and sink from view, while fellow workers would simply stand and gaze. Questions why no efforts were made to save the man would bring out a laconic answer, "He no my family!"

A burial was a real celebration, and funerals ranged from productions rivaling the best efforts of Mafia gangster over-lords to the super-economy type where everything, including the coffin, was rented – in the case of the coffin, for one year's-tenancy. With a wealthy Chinese or high dignitary, official parking would be delayed for months until a propitious combination of sun, moon and stars could be determined by soothsayers and astrologers. In the meantime, a gorgeously decorated catafalque, the size of a small house, was prepared to contain the coffin in the funeral procession. A crew of as many as two hundred men was required to carry the structure, with an intricate system of rigging and cross-rigging, allowing each individual bearer to carry his full share of the weight. Moving at a shuffling and steady pace, the crew would halt on signal ... each bearer would put a long heavy stick in place which, with some help, would hold up the catafalque while the bearers took a breather or did anything else considered necessary.

White was the color of mourning. White clad friends and relatives marched on foot in the procession, numbers augmented by scores of paid professional mourners. The higher the pay, the louder the moans and wails, and the wilder the sounds of paid musicians, whose special discords eventually became the basis of modern rock music. Money would be needed to pay off and pacify possible demons or devils encountered en route. So little disks of golden or silver foil paper were thrown among the spectators lining the funeral way.

To provide the deceased with a small snack on the way, trays of food – meats, fruits, candies – would be borne along in the procession and later deposited on the gigantic grave mound. The deceased were apparently heavy eaters, as the masses of food piled on the grave were mysteriously gone by dawn of the next day, taken either by spirits or passersby.

In addition to food offerings and paper money, there were papier-mâché figures of horses and servants for celestial transport, and gaily dressed female figures placed on the tomb, intended as symbolic concubines for the departed. Upon arrival at the appointed place in the cemetery there would be a crescendo of noise: more fireworks, beating tom-toms and frenzied shouts and moans by the paid mourners. The coffin was removed from the catafalque, placed in a deep hole, and then covered with an enormous mound of dirt some fifteen to twenty feet high. When the various offerings, including the food supplies, were placed on the mound, the assembled mourners, paid and unpaid, would quietly slip away, thoroughly exhausted from the celebration A few of the smarter spectators watched carefully where the choicest food gifts were placed, with the idea of returning late at night and beating celestial spirits to the free lunch.

Common burials were much simpler. A heavy wood casket was carried by four to six bearers: the white-clad relatives, with usually two screaming and crying professional mourners, a few strips of tinsel thrown along the way, and trays of elderly vegetables and rice as provisions for lunch on the Styx crossing. The coffin, to provide for easy later recovery and re-use, was buried only a few feet under the surface.

Tientsin is practically at sea level and occasional floodings would bring coffins to the surface. This happening, especially with the older graves, resulted in an unusual ground rule on the score cards of the Tientsin Golf Club: "A ball, lying in an open grave or coffin, may be lifted and dropped without penalty." Towering old grave mounds, cut off at the top, also made excellent tees for several of the holes, and empty graves, excellent traps.

There was no actual desecration in the use of the old cemetery which extended for miles inland and along the river. In the ancient days, with a change in dynasty, all of the cemeteries throughout the land were cleared, leveled and the land given back to food production. With the last dynasty change, ending the rule of the Empress Dowager in 1911, the new government was too weak to risk possible opposition to the clearing of the burial areas, so that hundreds of square miles remained uncared for and unused.

For many years following the Dowager, the new government was a muddled semi-democracy: a powerless President with a mere shadow cabinet. Hoards of clerks and functionaries, operating under the Empress, were slid quietly into similar positions under the President. There was no Pentagon to incur the wrath of newspaper pundits, and fortunately no television. The general public mind was made up or down by various warlords, each one operating for his own personal benefit and with his own private army. At stated periods there would be an election, and with high offices it was a recognized practice to pay for votes. In the case of block votes, payment was often made by check, usually postdated after election day, to insure results. Watergate-type practices were unknown. Nevertheless, the country functioned without particular difficulty, as lack of communications and distance kept the various provinces completely uninformed as to affairs and conditions in neighboring or distant provinces.

Vast sums due from the government as indemnity to both the British and United States governments for the Boxer Rebellion were turned over for scholarship purposes to provide education for the upper class and, apparently, more intelligent Chinese youth. In England, this education was Rhodes Scholarships; in the USA, similar grants at leading Eastern Universities. The intention was to provide a reservoir of young Chinese trained in government and industry.

Actually the results were meager. Students would return to the homeland, enthused and starry-eyed. The Rhodes Scholars wore monocles and were avid for cricket; the U.S. contingents wore college button caps and chewed gum. Both groups were unrecognized by foreigners and not accepted by the homeland. As enthusiasm faded, the greater majority slowly returned to the old indolent way and custom of cumshaw, concubines, and squeeze as a way of life.

There was a fable related by Putnam Wiel, famous Chinese expert and historian:

In the days of the Empire, the Emperor, having heard vaguely of lighted streets in the capitals of foreign powers, called in his Chancellor, presented him with a million taels in cash taken from his personal funds, and directed him to see that the city streets of Peking were adequately lighted. After a series of thankful bows, the Chancellor called in the Keeper of the Privy Seal and announced that Old Man had kicked in with a half million from his personal funds to light the streets of Peking – gradually cut down to some thousand taels. The Mayor pocketed the balance and issued an order that each householder would provide a lantern before his gateway – and the streets of Peking were lit!

As a Company Commander and later Operations Officer of the 15th Infantry Regiment with the motto "Can do!" I was particularly involved in a program heavily stressing sports and athletics, with the aim of keeping the local military mind off popular indoor games.

Polo, a sport now strictly confined to maharajahs, millionaires' sons, horse traders and cowboys, was financially possible in the early China, days, even for poorly paid army officers. Instead of multi-thousand-priced thoroughbreds, mounts in China were limited to native Mongolian ponies ... stout, stocky and bull-necked. Once a year, bands of shaggy, untrained three-year-olds would be brought from the plains of Hailar to the spring horse auctions in Tientsin and

Peking. Under an agreement originally made by the British, a height limit of 14 hands (4 foot 8 inches) at the withers was established to prevent working in of bigger crossbreeds, A second agreement, violently protested by the Mongolian horse dealers but held to by foreign buyers, was a limit on the original purchase price: fifty dollars or the equivalent. This custom left the future development of the pony up to the player and not his banker. Strings of fifteen to twenty ponies were not uncommon, to be worked on until the mounts showed good handling ability and speed, otherwise they were peddled for cart usage. A "mafoo," or groom, caring for three ponies would be paid around $3.00 per month with tacit permission to eat part of the horses' grain ration.

With this balance in size and price, competition was keen. The height limit made cut-down mallets necessary, and the boot soles of long-legged riders would almost touch the ground. But the speed, the bump, and the thrill of a clean hit were still there. Tournaments held in Tientsin, Shanghai, and Peking played to packed grandstands, both with white and Chinese.

A special hazard at Tientsin was that the playing field was inside the main race course, separated by a narrow but deep moat. The hazard was when a hard-mouthed pony would race directly for the moat, the water being an ecologist's nightmare.

A second traditional ground rule developed over the years. It involved any player spilled from his mount, unless the pony also went down. The jarred victim would be met at the sideboards by a grinning white-jacketed bar-boy, bearing on a silver platter one drink – usually a gimlet – and a chit to be signed covering a drink for each club member present in the clubhouse. A cagey player soon learned to trip the pony as he went down, especially when the clubhouse was crowded.

Flat racing with pari-mutuel betting, with abacus calculations speedier than computers, was the most popular sport, foreign and native.

A weekly program of flat racing and one steeplechase over narrow ditches and mini-hurdles, jammed stands to capacity. Entrance tickets for the semi-annual "Championships" were scalped at terrific prices months before the event. To secure so-called "gentlemen jockeys," in other words, "non-Chinese," the minimum weight limit imposed was 150 pounds. This made the hunched-up jockey seat impracticable, but the stands would cheer wildly as the jockeys with long flailing legs would boot their mounts toward the finish line.

Track and football were popular but limited in participation: our Marine rivals from Peking, the French, and the English. The top event of the track season was the Annual Bastille Day Meet at the French Arsenal. Performance-wise, the events were bush-league, except for the Tug-of-War. Our entry invariably consisted of a team of over-muscled, overweight mess sergeant types, matched against a team of tiny, wiry French Annamite soldiers. David vs. Goliath! Beer vs. brains! With the whistle, our ponderous machine would slowly drag the lightweight rivals towards the center line, speed decreasing as sweat increased, then a flashy tactic change by the French: lying back with rigid bodies and dug-in cleats as our gallant behemoths puffed and tugged ... another whistle signal ... the pressure relaxed for a second. Then each man spun the rope over his shoulder and, with machine-like steps and precision, would drag our heavyweights over the line. This same crushing defeat had happened year after year. When I asked the French coach just what his soldiers did for training in this event, he took me around to an old brick wall. In the shelter of the wall were four complete teams straining and tugging for ten minutes at a time on ropes fastened to old railroad springs embedded in concrete.

My favorite track event, the broad – now the long – jump, was a little-better. With the French and English jumpers doing around twenty feet, the competition was no particular problem.

The main difficulty was with the merchandise prizes given by the French, which varied widely. A case of good champagne might be given for third place and an atrocious ormolu French clock for first. After looking over the display, I would jump easily until the final jump and then put a small white marker to hit with my foot, to insure the required first, second or third prize.

Football was another limited effort – a three-game season, twice against the Peking Marines and once against a Shanghai civilian team. To keep in shape and to piece out a season, several of us went over to the British with the idea of playing Rugby. I had seen the game while at Stanford and had only a very general idea. The first game was against the French. The British Captain decided that I would be OK at wing, a somewhat similar position to end where I played in our football.

Just before the game he approached me and remarked, "Art, old fellow! Just a few points. If an opponent comes at you with the intention of impeding your progress, it is perfectly permissible if you fend him off with your free hand!" This seemed logical. When the ball came out of the scrum and was picked up by our half and lateraled out until it finally arrived in my hands, I really got my big feet moving. Cutting in, I saw ahead of me the French halfback, Lefarve (who was later to be a general in the French army), with his arms held wide out. Thinking of my instructions, I shifted the ball to my left arm, spun and delivered a perfect straight arm directly under his chin.

He was screaming, "Foul!" before he hit the ground. Our team captain dashed up. "No, No! Merely fend at them, old fellow!" I apologized. Many years later we met again in North Africa.

Baseball was our one great sport – popular, but not played by the Chinese. In my college days, we had been against the leading college teams of Japan: Keio, Moeji, and Waseda. At that time the Japanese were excellent fielders and base runners but were puff ball hitters. Outfielders would play just back of the infield to get some part of the action. But under instruction of American big-leaguers, baseball had flourished in every way: college teams on a par with a good semi-pro team; and the professional Japanese team, the Tokyo Giants, were as good as a good AA team, in addition to being tall and big. With our U.S. rivals, the 31st Infantry of Manila and the Marines, our season was terrific. Game after game to crowded stadiums ... Chinese spectators blandly wondering ... British spectators politely remarking, "Damn well stroked, old man," ... and our own fans.

In British-American interest, golf was the leading sport. So-called "Hong" matches between business firms and clubs were monthly affairs, with the Army entered as a separate unit. The old graveyard course itself was unique, especially with its ground rule of "ball in an open grave or coffin can be lifted and dropped without penalty." Except during the rainy season when there was a sparse cover of rough grass, the fairways were smooth, with a constantly cultivated cover of fine earth. Each green, also of dirt, was in the charge of a special greens keeper. Underneath were layers of coarse rock, then successively finer gravel, permitting drainage, then a top dressing of powdered soil, giving the same playing feel as that of an excellent grass green. Ball marks or foot marks were immediately smoothed out after play.

Carts were unknown and unnecessary. Each player had two caddies, one a club carrier and the other ranging far out in front to spot and mark the ball with a flag. There were rumors that the barefooted caddies, ranging around in the rough, might occasionally improve a lie with an agile toe. However, as everyone gambled in China, even if it was a mere tenth of the cent, caddies always had money riding on their employer. This would be noticed. One thing true of the caddies on both sides: when a ball would land in a trap or bunker, a gleeful shout of "Go Li La" would greet the event.

Face being important in China, it was considered bad form if the player in any way had to handle his ball. Prior to starting out on the first tee, the player would indicate to his club-carrying caddie the exact height that his ball should be teed up. From a small can of clay the caddy would then shape a rough tee in his mouth, place it on the ground with the correct height, set the ball, and move back. It was considered very low class to even pick up your ball from the hole.

With the normal shallow lies, an iron was an extremely important club, with the "midiron," or present No. 2 iron, much used. When I first arrived in China, I brought with me something absolutely new in golf clubs: a steel-shafted midiron! For two years, until several more steel shafted clubs appeared, this was very much frowned upon. "Nothing like the old wooden shaft, you know." ... "Typical Yankee modernism." In formal tournaments the steel shafted club was barred.

The caliber of golf played was, for the period, extremely good. In team matches I was paired for three years- with Lawson Little. This was not the later golf champion Lawson Little, Jr., but his father, Lt. Col. Lawson Little, U.S. Army. Lawson Jr. at that time didn't know a diaper from a driver. Lawson Sr. was an extremely steady and consistent player. I was occasionally erratic and occasionally brilliant. But between us we managed to snare the Hong Championship for three years.

Life wasn't all sport and amusement for the occupational forces. Each year rival warlords, Chang Tso Lin and Wu Bei Fu, would engage in their annual civil war. Maneuvers were ritualistic. Chang, warlord of the areas north of the Great Wall, would bring his troops on the government railroad to a battle position approximately two hundred miles south of Tientsin. Wu, warlord of Central China, would then bring his troops northward to the battle area using the same government railroad. Both armies were dressed in the same gray cotton uniforms with wrapped, leggings and soft floppy hats. Equipment also included an umbrella, not really needed as all battles would be automatically stopped and postponed in event of rain. Distinguishing insignia was a blue armband for the Chiang forces and a red armband for the Wu troops, with the smart ones carrying a spare of each color.

Ammunition added to the general confusion. After the Russian-Japanese War in 1905, vast quantities of small arms ammunition, both Japanese and Russian, had been gathered and stored in great warehouses or "go-downs" in various parts of North China, ostensibly under supervision of an Inter-Allied Commission. Annual checks had been made until matters became so routine that everything behind a towering front row of ammunition boxes had long been removed and sold to various warlords or other militarists. This made everyone happy, excepting one bad feature: over the years the ammunition had gradually deteriorated until, to fire a cartridge, it was necessary to point the rifle up in the air, then jam it down against a shoulder to bring the remaining powder against the primer. It would usually explode with satisfactory war-like noises but didn't make for excellent marksmanship.

Once in battle position, the rival forces would meet in combat, shoot off as much ammunition as would explode, then rest up. Meantime the rival paymasters would arrive with the respective payrolls, consisting of several freight cars loaded with metal "cash," a round Chinese coin with a hole in the middle, usually worn in a string around the neck, with a value of approximately one one-hundredth of a cent. The rest period was also hard on the steam locomotives, as nearby soldiers would use the hot water for their tea.

Following several clashes with rest periods in between, Chiang, feeling he was overextended, would start his slow retreat to the North, naturally using the government railway. I recall a terrific artillery barrage by the Wu forces endeavoring to knock out a small wooden bridge, after giving Chiang plenty of time to use it in his retreat. After five hours shelling at medium range, the bridge was still intact, and also usable for Wu's pursuing forces.

It was only when Chiang's retreating army reached the vicinity of Tientsin that the Allied forces would come into the picture to insure that both armies would be shunted past the foreign concession areas in Tientsin, en route to the next traditional halt, Tongshan, a small city close to the vast coal mines of the Kailan Mining Administration, directly between the two rival armies. There was possible danger of destruction should a real battle occur.

I was summoned by Colonel Martin.

McChrystal, you will go to Tongshan with appropriate forces that will later be augmented by British troops. Your force will occupy the Tongshan area with the specific mission of keeping peace between Chiang Tso Lin and Wu Bei Fu and to protect foreign lives and property. In addition I want to warn you against bringing on a military engagement unless it is necessary to save human lives.

When I discovered that my force would consist of a sergeant and two squads of American soldiers to "be later increased by a detachment of Sikhs from the 55th, with Koks Rifles," I mentally decided that any military engagement would be very carefully considered.

There were several special things in connection with the assigned task. For the first time in my life I had a private train, admittedly only a locomotive, flat car and a small passenger car, but a private train, and we departed from Tientsin with appropriate ceremony. Arriving a few miles north, we found Wu's troops sprawled over the right of way. My force, all fifteen, smartly uniformed, were aligned back-to-back on the flat car, with a machine gun mounted at each end. The detachment was brought to attention and a salute given as we passed a large tent, apparently Wu's headquarters. Then we cleared the track of slumbering or sitting soldiers by the simple expedient of blasting the whistle and slowly moving along the track, as they jumped for safety. At Tongshan, we left the main line and proceeded down the mining company spur track to the company offices. There we established ourselves in a small mess usually used by the upper company staff, and proceeded to set up radio communications with the U.S. Headquarters. A complete housekeeping crew was furnished by the company together with a most satisfactory array of edibles and a few excellent drinkables. I could see possibilities in being an Allied Commander.

Early the next morning there arrived a detachment of 36 Sikh soldiers under command of Subadar Major Singh, be-whiskered and be-medaled. A British officer, accompanying the detachment, indicated Singh would be in charge of the British and gave me a few Indian words, including "Yes, Ho, Come, Go, Water, Food." He suggested use of sign language for the rest, and then gaily departed.

As I moved towards my new force, they were called to attention by the Subadar. I stood at attention as they rendered what I considered was an extremely military salute. To my surprise, the Subadar deprecatingly waved me back, turned around and proceeded to raise hell and had the group perform several practice salutes. Finally he was satisfied. I moved again to the front of the detachment, and this time, when the salute was given, you could hear the slap of slings and the click of heels for blocks.

His English vocabulary was somewhat limited except for military subjects, but we had no further difficulty – perfect rapport by sign language and gestures, pieced with a few words. He was one of the really wonderful soldier types of the old Indian army.

From one of our sign language conferences came my decision that the Indian complement would be used for protection of the camp and the property, and the U.S. contingent would be used for continued saluting and ceremonial duties.

There were many problems occasioned by my own ignorance and unfamiliarity with their customs. I had the carpenters for the mining company prepare a well-constructed "12-holer" military-type latrine to receive word, through gesture and sign language, that each hole would have to be curtained off according to Indian usage.

The principle article of food was goat meat and they brought a large herd of goats, very plump and very smelly. Wandering around, and watching the native cooks preparing what looked like over-sized griddle cakes, I suddenly noticed that one of the cakes was picked up and thrown away. Then with a complicated exchange of signs I realized that, as an unbeliever, I had allowed my shadow to fall on the cake, rendering it impure.

Another slight problem was entirely handled by my friend the Subadar. It appeared that a portion of his command didn't drink, another portion didn't smoke, and a third portion did everything. One thing was certain – they could fight if necessary.

Another new situation was that the Indian complement included "bearers of water." As the nearest natural water source was a spring some five miles away, the Subadar and I decided on a solution which involved bringing a water tank car to the vicinity of the camp and letting it drip slightly to get the natural effect of a shower.

I spent a month with my friend, the Subadar, and his detachment. I sensed their pride in being soldiers, even if the place as a soldier was a "bearer of water." As we started, daily trips along the rail line, from Chiang's headquarters to the headquarters of Wu, I increased the saluting contingent to fourteen from each nation, and we would shake up the slovenly Chinese headquarters in each village. Finally the word came: Wu was returning south the next day. Chiang was moving north back of the Wall.

That night there was a quiet, almost wordless celebration between Subadar Major Singh and Allied Commander Captain McChrystal. Little was I thinking that in less than two decades I would again be associated with Indian troops in Italy.

It was with mixed emotions that, in the Fall of 1925, I received orders to proceed to Fort Benning, Georgia, the Infantry School, as a member of the Instructional Regiment, the 29th Infantry.

It had been a wonderful four years of exotic living, sport and adventure. But the breaking-up signs of the Old China Hand days were clearly visible. Korea, bursting with population hordes; the adjoining unpopulated desert lands of Mongolia, there for the taking by Japanese forces. A bold holdup of the "Blue Express," Peking-bound, with the holding of British and American hostages, including women, would have never occurred during the long years of British control. In the major cities were scowls barely concealed, mutterings of *"fung guai"* ("foreign devil"); heavy and unabashed increases in graft and *"cumshaw"* (a gratuity or tip as thanks for a service) by merchants, employees and officials.

In a professional way there also had been many changes. The powerful U.S. Forces in China with its 750 officers and men had done well under a Colonel or occasionally a Lt. Colonel with a small Headquarters staff. But in peacetime, places must be found for unemployed Generals and China was no exception. Early in 1925 a complete new command setup arrived, headed by Brigadier General William D. Conner with two aides, four General Staff Officers, a Chaplain; assorted orderlies; and, while not on the table of organization, Mrs. Brigadier General. While unrated in the command echelon, Mrs. B.G. was loaded financially, as her ancestors had developed a highly popular "female complaint" remedy guaranteed to cure something, and with a high alcoholic content, positive to please, it was financially remunerative.

Without background inquiry the new command took positive steps to eliminate "cupid's catarrh" (V.D.) and similar ailments. An Official Order was issued to the effect that "All forms of illicit sexual intercourse will cease, effective 8:00 a.m. tomorrow morning, by order of the Commanding General."

With this proving ineffective, a punitive approach was tried. An enlisted member of the command, contracting V.D., would be court-martialed, given six months' forfeiture of pay and allowances, and reduced to grade of private. Company Commanders, fully appreciating the conditions faced by unmarried soldiers, wholeheartedly supported any practical move to cut down the rate of venereal disease. But all, to the man, protested against the court-martial method, especially reduction to private. These were the days when a man would normally have ten to twelve years' service before being promoted to corporal. With no change in the announced order it was not uncommon to find old-time non-coms on special leave during inspection days, provided that he was taking treatments from reliable German specialists.

My entanglement with the new command was purely personal, not military. For several weeks I had been on the target range below the Great Wall at Shanikwan working with the regimental team on my favorite weapon, the 45 automatic. When I returned to Tientsin I was informed that Mrs. Brigadier General had been making some rather pointed remarks concerning my wife and the fact that she had gone out socially during my absence.

Not being an over-disciplined West Pointer and, from experience, not being greatly in awe of General Officers in peacetime, I went directly to General Connor and informed him as to what had been said by Mrs. General. I further notified him that he would shut her mouth, or that I, Captain McChrystal, would take steps to see it was shut. He stated that the affair was regrettable and that he would do what was possible. (Note: This was years before Martha Mitchell.) Later I was to suffer many uncomfortable months due to this incident.

There was the usual round of farewells. Good-bye to the Ambassador in Peking and a farewell party with the Marine Staff and members of the various athletic teams; farewell to Major Joe Stillwell, in Peking as a language student and later to become "Vinegar Joe," victim of the Long March from Bataan; farewell to Billy Riley, USMC, later to become a large figure in United Nation affairs.

All household furniture was packed, and we gave the traditional "crate tea." All officers of the garrison, their wives and friends were invited. The General was invited but was apparently engaged. The principal decoration was long rows of partly full bottles, incapable of being transported to the homeland, with bottles numbered one to nine. Incoming guests were called on to choose numbers, serial numbers, which would result in a mild or wild mixture of some four or five different types. As bottles were emptied they would be replaced, entirely changing the order.

By late evening most of the guests, would be gone ... also unresponsive. A courteous gesture was distribution at the door of small bottles of Alka-Seltzer, famous even in those days.

Three events occurred just before our departure. The Fifteenth won the Championship of the Orient; my second son, Richard Gregory, was born; and I was warned by the Chief of Staff that Connor was gunning for me.

Arriving in San Francisco, we created a mild sensation with the children walking serenely with their Chinese nurses, conversing loudly in Chinese, then switch-hitting to English. My shock was at the old Palace Hotel when I ordered a bottle of whiskey from the Bell Captain. "Twenty-five dollars"... (eighty cents in China).

At Fort Benning I reported for duty with the Demonstration Regiment... 29th Infantry. After a year as Instructor I finally took the Company Officer's Course. Actually I did quite well.

Arthur J. McChrystal

5. THE BATTLE OF BRITAIN

to "Torch," 1940-1943

War was news in 1940 … big news … grim news. It was someone else's war, far, far away. It was October, 1940, and I was still living in San Francisco running two shows, the "Ice Frolics" and the "Wheel of Fortune," at the Golden Gate International Exposition which was running for its second time in the city that year. Besides being in show business I also held the position of Vice President of the S.F. Downtown Association. Both jobs were keeping me really busy, to say the least.

I received a call one day while I was at work from General Emory S. "Hank" Adams who informed me that with the consent of the British I had been selected by the State Department and the War Department to go to the Court of St. James, London, as a Political Advisor to Ambassador Joseph Kennedy. I thought about this offer long and hard. I had to consider my many responsibilities in the city. Fortunately for me, should I decide to accept this job offer from the military, there were only a few weeks left before the fair [Treasure Island Fair: Golden Gate International Exposition, 1939-1940] would be closing and my two shows would come to an end. As for my position as the Vice President of the San Francisco Downtown Association, it would be a matter of just stepping down, and that I did. I had made up my mind to accept the position as the Political Advisor for Ambassador Joseph Kennedy. It took me a few weeks to wrap up all my affairs in the city. With the blessings and approval of my family and friends I was soon on my way to Washington D.C.

Upon my arrival at the Washington D.C. airport I was met by military personnel who provided me with a staff car for my transportation and my reservations for the very crowded Mayflower Washington Hotel. There were two solid days of conferences and meetings that

I needed to attend with General "Hank" Adams, General Crane Carlton Magruder of G-2 and General Sumner Welles of the State Department. I realized the organizational impact of General Hank Adam's remark at one of our conferences at the point when I was informed that in addition to being a Political Advisor to Ambassador Kennedy I was to be the Executive Officer of the Military Attachés Office with the mission of converting the office from a peacetime operation to an office prepared for possible wartime status. I was given repeated briefings, a passport, money and instructions on secret papers and code handling. There were several press interviews that had been arranged for me which I was required to attend before I would be able to depart on my trip to London.

In the morning on October 20th I boarded a Pan Am Clipper flight at the Washington D.C. airport, bound for England with a few stops along the way in order to refuel the plane for our long flight. We landed in New York briefly and then we were on our way to our second destination, Bermuda. From Bermuda the plan was to fly to Horta Bay and then on to Lisbon. With a few changes of transport we would eventually arrive in London. After five hours of flight time we were over Bermuda; the blackout curtains of the plane were drawn to prevent spying on the defenses in the area or the many rooftop sunbathers.

Upon landing in Bermuda we were instructed to remain near the plane so that we would be ready to embark as soon as the refueling was finished. There were nine passengers total and we were all anxious to complete the journey to our final destination, London. As we waited to board the plane we were told that there was going to be a slight delay. My how plans can change! It was more than a slight delay: we were in Bermuda for fourteen days. As it turned out, the swells in Horta Bay, Azores, were over three feet and dangerous for a clipper landing. The nine of us would be spending the next fourteen days at the luxurious and leisurely Belmont Manor and Golf Club with all of our expenses paid for by good old Pan Am, except for our personal bar bill. Bermuda was a beautiful, sleepy and an easy-going island with eight wonderful golf courses including the Mid-Ocean Golf Course. Bicycles were the primary vehicle of transportation for the bow-legged natives who rode around the streets at a casual pace. There were only two motor vehicles on the island, a car belonging to the Governor and the local city fire engine.

On the second day of my stay in Bermuda another clipper arrived on the island unexpectedly. It was a special flight from London via Lisbon with Ambassador Kennedy and his family. Uncle Joe had apparently gotten tired of waiting for me and all my advice that I had for him as his Political Advisor. It would be twelve more days until we would be able to leave the island for Horta Bay because of the current harsh weather conditions that persisted. Each day I spent with the Kennedy family was pleasant and fairly routine. There were morning sails on the beautiful bays of Bermuda, shore picnics, rounds of golf and plenty of time to just sit around engaged in conversation or merely enjoying island life. By the time our departure day had arrived, the romantic attachments of the island life had waxed and waned. Bermuda, with all its beauty, had become a little tiresome after a while. I was anxious to get to London and get to work.

The Kennedy family and I boarded the clipper for an evening flight. The nighttime take-off in the clear moonlight was absolutely breathtaking, as was the landing in Horta Bay that next morning. What a beautiful bay hamlet with a dominant volcano (Capelinhos Volcano) in the distance! We were there about an hour, just long enough for the refueling of the flying boat and the refueling of the passengers with hot coffee and excellent Portuguese brandy. The take-off of the clipper was a bit bouncy but apparently safe. Our next destination was the Tagus River, Lisbon. Upon our arrival it was necessary for all of us to go through the Immigration and the Customs check points. We were safely passed through the check points with our diplomatic immunity and the guidance of Andrew Jackson Kelly, the Pan Am Station Agent for Lisbon who later became the Pan Am Vice President for all of Europe. Our next flight would be at 3:30 a.m. from the Sintra Airport bound for Bournemouth; this time we would be flying on a BOAC plane. We spent our remaining few hours before our departure indulging in the conventional Portuguese sport, hot coffee and excellent brandy.

The flight from Lisbon to Bournemouth was calm and uneventful except for my slight hangover and two sudden detours into nearby cloud banks when unidentified aircrafts appeared in the distance. We arrived in Bournemouth briefly and then we were on our way to Portsmouth. After we disembarked the plane at the Portsmouth Airport we were required once again to go through the Immigration and Customs formalities. From the airport we headed to the train station, where we caught a ride to London. There was a short wait before we could board our train, so we decided to enjoy a spot of English tea, instead of the usual coffee and brandy. Our arrival date to London just so happened to coincide with the last of the daylight raids by the Goering boys during which some hundred odd planes were shot down, each one apparently falling in our direction. This was enough to keep me on edge. We arrived at Victoria Station where an Embassy car was waiting to take Colonel Latrobe, two code-expert sergeants and myself to No. 1 Grosvenor Square, the American Embassy.

The Embassy site, Grosvenor Square, had a small red brick building on one of the corners. There were plans to build more structures over the entire square, including a monstrous American Eagle statue. Facing the wrought iron fencing of the park square were mostly luxury apartment houses, with the exception of the Japanese Embassy and the mounds of rubble from the two demolished buildings that had been destroyed by bombs. As I entered the Embassy I noticed that it was surprisingly quiet; the only people there were the Duty Officer and some cleaning woman. I proceeded to sign the register and the Duty Officer showed me the office that was to be mine. I decided to have a look at the main clerical offices, finding that the only sign of activity was the overflowing of paper in the desk baskets. A general air of disorder surrounded me. There was one desk that had a small wooden plaque on the top of it which read "Miss Lowe." Of all the surrounding offices, this was the only desk that was neat and clear. I was wondering where everyone was. I thought there might have been a sudden air raid and the personnel had taken cover. I located the Duty Officer and asked him where everyone was. He replied to me with a touch of hauteur in his voice, "Today is Saturday, Sir! No one comes on Saturday!" This was my introduction to the "German Secret Weapon." It was the "British Weekend"!

I left the Embassy and was off to check in at Claridge's hotel, home to the kings and queens and to the maharajahs and millionaires. This was my temporary home until I could locate a modest flat. The hotel was beautiful, despite the disfigured sandbags that were stacked high in front of the entrance and the plate glass windows. Should a bomb fall outside the hotel, the sandbags were there to keep the glass and the doorman from being blown into the lobby. The front desk clerk informed me that all the arrangements had already been made and the rent for my apartment would be at a special price. I was taken majestically upwards in a bronze mirrored deck lift to the floor where my apartment was and then ushered into my modest quarters.

The apartment was a large corner room on the top floor with a magnificent view of London in two directions. The furniture was beautiful; there were twin beds, a bathroom with a black and white tiled tub slightly smaller than a swimming pool and an essential piece of equip.m.ent resembling a royal throne; three walk-in closets which were ample space for my suitcases; a very plush easy chair and a dressing table with mirrors suitable for Marie Antionette. Mentally I was hoping that the "special price" would be 95% off the list price. As the attendant unpacked my meager belongings I decided to check the various switches in the room, which all seemed to be working. Feeling properly rewarded I settled down into the soft easy chair. I was home at last in London and to hell with the price of the apartment. It was worth it!

I was so tired that first night in my apartment that if there was an air-raid I didn't hear it. I had caused a commotion almost as chaotic as an air-raid at 8 o'clock that next morning when I went downstairs to eat breakfast in the dining room instead of having it delivered to my room, which was the current wartime rule. I wish someone had informed me of that rule! I won't make that mistake again! After all the excitement I had lost my appetite and decided to head to my new office which was a few blocks away from my apartment. I passed by a number of people on the way to the Embassy; most of them were Sunday church goers streaming towards the Farm Street Church which was near the Square.

I arrived at the Embassy to find another Duty Officer at the registration desk who asked me for my identification. After receiving my clearance I went upstairs to the main offices to see who might be around. There was no Mr. Johnson, Charge d'Affairs, present in the first office. I glanced into the office of General Raymond Lee's, the Military Attaché. He was not there either. Let me guess, the British don't work on Sundays as well as Saturdays. I went to the clerical desk, which was the only desk that I'd noted the day before that was totally clean and organized. Lo and behold, there was a neatly dressed young lady sitting at the desk. "I'm Miss Lowe, Major!" she remarked. "You are my new secretary," I replied. From that day on until I left for North Africa in 1943 Miss Lowe was my right hand secretary. Her work was absolutely excellent.

It was my first day at my new job and I went right to work. I checked the various standing orders, assignments and office procedures. It was around 11:00 a.m. when an individual showed up in my office. He had a ruddy face with a bristling moustache and was wearing a sweater and white trousers and swinging a cased tennis racquet. With a gleaming smile he said, "Welcome McChrystal! I'm Raymond Lee and I'm glad you're here!" We chatted for over an hour in his office about the imminent situation and what should be done in order to convert the modestly-staffed peacetime operation into a fast-moving intelligence outfit, geared for war. There was no doubt in Lee's mind that we would eventually be involved in the war. He particularly liked the fact that I was "Retired Military" so that I could step on toes without worrying about any recourse. As he left he saluted me with his tennis racquet and said to me, "The office is yours, young fellow! Run it as you like! I'll be the Military Attaché!" That was how it remained until a year later when Lee left to attend a conference and to take some leave time for Christmas in the USA. The office situation had remained fairly normal during peacetime when I first arrived in London. Ambassadors were being selected in direct ratio to their political contributions. A Military Attaché required an outside job in direct ratio to the desirability of the particular post. The court of St. James, London, received the highest rating along with two South American countries and Paris, which were grouped for a second rating. Ambassadorial expenses were well covered but it didn't hurt to have a well-loaded wife. The up-keep of a Military Attaché's office was covered through G-2 but the budget was negligible until the bombing of Pearl Harbor.

I began to reorganize the office with the able assistance of Miss Lowe in preparation for a wartime scenario. I first changed the office hours, which were to be 9 a.m. to noon, a two-hour break, and then 2 p.m. to 5 p.m. daily, including the unheard of requirement of working Saturdays from 9 a.m. until noon. Transatlantic calls were to be written out ahead of time and clocked. Cables were sent on the basis that the sender was to pay for them personally. There had been a Senior Officer who had been constantly cabling daily resumes of articles from the London newspapers at twenty cents per word when this material was already available at any of the World Press Agencies. The Officer claimed that it was primarily a recheck for press accuracy.

My job wasn't made any easier by the German Luftwaffe's dropping of bombs at frequent intervals. Before too long everything started to change at the Embassy, as we planned for the wartime scenario. There was a tremendous amount of questioning that came from various civilians in the area wanting to know about the detailed plans that had been enacted for the engagement of war. One afternoon I heard a remark from Miss Falby, a graduate from one of the finest schools in England for young ladies. Miss Falby seemed to be passionate about helping in this wartime situation in London and when she entered the Embassy she didn't hesitate to make demands for information. "Where in HELL are those Goddam files?" she shouted. Since this demand was not directed at me I wasn't exactly sure what files she was demanding. However I was impressed with her assertiveness. I began to have hope that in fact the people of London were willing to engage in their own way to help out with the cause.

As I saw more of General Lee I realized the bowler hat, the umbrella, the moustache, and the "Anglicized" appearance was mostly an excellent cover for one of the best intelligence minds in the intelligence business. Lee was a soldier, diplomat, philosopher and a friend with the rare ability of appreciating viewpoints other than his own, both personal and national. And he had the equally rare ability of reconciling those viewpoints with those of his own country. What success I had later on in England and during wartime in the vital field of allied cooperation and understanding was due greatly to the example and influence of this great American. He could also speak up if required. When I asked him about the departed Ambassador Kennedy, he remarked that Kennedy had the "smartness of a speculator" together with the "sharpshooting and facile insensitivity to the great forces now playing like heat lighting over the map of the world." After Kennedy returned to the USA he apparently had given only damn-fool interviews. Lee's advice to me as a newcomer to the London Blitz was, "This is the time to wear life like a loose garment."

Another character in London was Tom Balfour, a hardy Scot who had remained with the Embassy since WWI and could be depended upon to do anything from providing extra rations to roof watching. As Tom was the Embassy Chief Fire Warden I convinced him to sign me up for fire-watching duty. This duty was not required but it gave me a chance, when a raid was on, to do something besides sitting around and waiting inside a shelter that probably wouldn't stop even a medium-sized bomb. Tom immediately secured me with a padded inner liner for my American type helmet that tightened up on impact, like modern football helmets. He dourly remarked, "Sir! If youse was to be hit by a hardboiled egg with that hat on you'd have a proper headache!" It seemed I was properly dressed for my night fire-watching duty with my new lined tin hat, heavy woolen scarf, a short seaman's jacket Tom dug up, plus a small flask of spirits, which was never amiss in London's fog.

During my first week in London the Italians got into the Bomb London act. On November 12, 1940, a force of eighteen bombers and sixty fighters attempted to bomb the Thames docks. The results were not encouraging for the Italians. The RAF had shot down twenty-five planes, only losing one of their own. Two of the shot down planes showed typical Italian preparedness: helmets, bayonets, ten bottles of Chianti, and a five-pound cheese for each crew member. On that same day of November 12th Ex-Ambassador Kennedy announced in Boston that "England was finished!" English torpedo planes hit the Italian fleet at Taranto, sinking three of their six battleships. To even out the week, the Luftwaffe devastated Coventry on the night of November 14th.

Daylight raiding had practically ceased by late fall 1940 and Goering had apparently decided that the plane losses were too high due to the RAF and the anti-aircraft bombardments. So he started the continuous night raids, except for when the weather conditions on the German side of the Channel made returning to their homeland hazardous and costly.

When darkness fell upon London there would be the long drawn out up-and-down cries of the sirens, woo…woo…woo…woo…, of the raid warning system. Minutes later you could hear the distant sounds of the coast defense guns firing. There were fingers of light from battery operated searchlights that would search the sky for the incoming attacks, occasionally pinning targets. Contrails would start build-ing up in the direction of the invaders and from above at 20,000 to 30,000 feet a grim and deadly battle was about to begin. As the RAF targeted the planes one could see them spinning helplessly towards earth which were often tracked by the searchlights.

Like planes, bombs have sound characteristics. Ordinary 100 lbs or 200 lbs bombs would make a slight whistling sound, and block-buster bombs made a heavy swishing sound. Both types of bombs had terrific explosions on impact. With a second of delay time bomb debris was flung high into the air and then returned to earth. There were incendiaries which were dropped by the basketful; they made a crackling sound similar to a stick being drawn along a wooden fence, followed by sharp explosions as they landed on rooftops or streets. Incendiaries have a vein along the side of the casing in order to keep them upright, allowing the pointed fuse to ignite the charge of thermite or phosphorus upon impact. Some of the most spectacu-lar bombs were the parachute-borne land mines. One was dropped high over the Hotel Savoy area. Searchlights picked up the incoming land mine, and with anti-air guns the sharp shooters plugged away in an attempt to explode it before impact. The efforts failed to explode the land mine and it slowly drifted down, landing on the embankment gardens near the Cleopatra Needle, with a terrific explosion. Fortu-nately there were only a few injuries from the explosion, however the impact was so great that the windows were shattered for blocks in the surrounding area.

Firebomb fighting was fairly simple if you could get to the fire quickly and smother the flames with the buckets of sand, which were stored on the rooftops for this very reason. Later on in the war the Germans added a small dash of highly explosive material to the bombs, mak-ing them harder to put out with the buckets of sand. One would have to be very careful dealing with this type of fire because it burned at a greater intensity. The buckets of sand were used for protection, a barrier to fight behind, as well as for putting out the fire.

Occasionally a fire-bomb would miss a rooftop and land on a side porch or a veranda, which would really take off in a blaze. In this situation, if the door to the flat was unable to be opened by force, one would have to rappel on a rope from the rooftop, occasionally having to jump a simple ten feet or so onto the porch landing, which was usually eight or nine stories from the ground. I speak of these techniques of firefighting because I personally fought fires such as these.

One of the real hazards in this war was not so much the Luftwaffe but the Defense system itself. Every park in the center of London had finally been equipped with rapid-firing rocket guns flinging hundreds of pieces of hardware into the sky in the general direction of the invading bombers, with occasional success. Due to the law of averages and the immutable law of physics, "What goes up must come down," that was the real danger! Because of this extreme danger, the roof watchers always clung closely to a heavy brick chimney or crouched low under a supposedly solid boundary wall if they could find one. The experienced fire-watchers, which I consider myself to be one of them, could accurately identify the type of bomb that was being dropped. "There's a Messerschmitt" was the call when there was an incoming light bomb, and "There's a Fokker" was the call when there was a fast bomb. I even learned to distinguish the sound of an incoming Heinkel bomb carrier plane which had two motors that ran slightly out of sync.

The night of December 30th, 1940 marked the four-hour Blitz on the City of London. I had taken the weekend off to be in the countryside near London when the Blitz began. I was able to observe the preliminary bombing and fires from afar. I had to return to London as quickly as possible, so I grabbed a cab at the Euston Station and headed for London, making a quick stop by my flat to get a heavy coat, a helmet and a bottle of restorer and then immediately went to where all the action was taking place. With my Embassy Pass I was able to get past the fire-lines, and that night I was a fireman for real! For four long hours the City of London was being blasted with big bombs, parachute bombs, oil bombs and incendiaries. The fires that were blazing in all directions of the City lit the target area for the bombers. It was just before midnight when the roar of planes overhead and the bombing suddenly ceased. According to later reports, heavy fog conditions developed on the German coast which made it dangerous for the returning aircraft to land safely. So there were orders issued to lift the attack and return home. Fires continued to blaze in London well into the following day. The destruction to the City was monumental! There were seven historic churches destroyed, which included the four built by Christopher Wren, the Guildhall, which was totally gutted, and St. Paul's Church, which was damaged but still stood tall and majestic amidst the ruins.

Bombing now became commonplace in England; war had become a way of life. Air-raid announcements would be made in the cinemas, theatres and other public places, giving directions to the nearest bomb shelter. When the announcements were made the crowds became very nervous and many began to cough as a reaction to the stress but very few people would leave for the shelter.

There was even rivalry that developed between various towns as to the amount of bomb damage each town had endured. In the small town of Cotswold there had been one firebomb which had burned a circle about fifty yards wide. The burned circle would quietly be retouched by the townspeople in order to keep the appearance of the original devastation to show that their town had also been bombed.

There was a lull from all the bombing, which had lasted almost three months. Then one day in the daylight hours sounds of a loud motor from a single engine plane could be heard. The motor of the plane suddenly cut out and the pilotless plane started spinning towards earth from about five thousand feet above with its impact-fused bomb. It was the V-1 missile. The V stood for "Vergeltungswaffen" (the German translation meaning weapons of reprisal). Another name for the missile (Fieseler Fi 103 V-1) was the Buzz Bomb or the Doodlebug.

What a shock it was to witness this new type of bomb, a day and night enemy warrior, after practically a bombing calm which we had experienced prior to this event. The RAF method of defense for these missiles was fairly successful. The defending pilots would fly along-side the incoming bombs and, with a deft flip, throw them off course which sent them spinning away from the main target. This technique was effective but hazardous for the defenders.

The next type of missile sent to the United Kingdom from the Germans was the V-2, the "Big Boy," and for the "bombie" it was the easiest of them all to deliver. This bomb traveled from The Hague to London, which was approximately 200 miles, in 5 minutes. It traveled so fast that it hit its target before you heard it, if you could even hear it. It was supersonic! The bombing of the liquid oxygen gas plant in Peenemunde by the RAF in the north-western part of Usedom (an island in the Baltic Sea off the coast of Germany) and their launching centers stopped both the V-1 and V-2 just in time.

Another assignment of mine, based on my propensity to talk and listen, was ambulance chasing. I followed the Luftwaffe all around England from Bournemouth to Manchester and beyond. After each raid I would dash to the scene in civilian clothing with my special police pass in order to interview as wide a cross section of people as possible. I would ask how they were feeling, how they were being handled and if they were going to move to the country or stick it out in the cities. My assignment brought me to all kinds of places, from Chambers of Lord Mayors to pubs, from bombed flat areas to burnt-out business districts, from slums to luxury estates. These were the places where I got British opinions. The people's answer to my question as to what they were going to do in this war-time scenario was usually a vague response, "Sometin' wud be done!" I would ask, "Do you think you're going to come out alright?" and lo and behold, from the top to the bottom, from hospitals to hovels within ruins, the answer was always, "Yes!" I watched and helped in the digging up of the wounded and the dead out of the ruins. There were rings of somber faces as the stretchers would pass by but there was never a word about quitting. That was the spirit!

Food conditions during the war were not especially bad for the average Brit except in quantity. Lord Woolton's gay governmental cookbook listed recipes for various goodies that were concocted from powdered eggs and powdered potatoes, a bit nauseating but filling. Seldom were there complaints about a meal as long as there was food on the table. As far as clothing for the people it was a matter of what one could afford or what one could make. The value of stocks grew less and less each day, which curbed spending in many ways even if was just for the basics.

In my time I've inspected Home Guard units with varying types of small arms, simulated cannons, simulated tanks and often simulated rations, but there was one thing that was never simulated and that was the plain guts of the people. When one thinks of the idea of installing oil pipelines along the beaches to be set ablaze in the event of an invasion, which had been a thought envisioned by a quiet English housewife, one must acknowledge the core participation of the English as a whole. Perhaps if the German leaders would have listened to their people when they had suggested not to engage in war, that would have been a smart idea.

Another assignment I had was the handling of various visiting firemen, officially called V.I.P.s, who thronged into London. The majority of the firemen were carrying personal letters from FDR and had at least three wishes, which were to have the opportunity to meet the Prime Minister, a visit to Dover and buying a Savile Row suit. Meeting the Prime Minister and acquiring a Savile Row suit was not a problem. The visit to Dover was usually resisted. The poor Dover garrison had to deal with the frequent visits of shells from the Krupp-made "Big Berta," a very large German gun, which was located in Calais, France, just across the English Channel.

My first V.I.P. encounter was with the tousle-headed Wendell Willkie. His visit to London came right after his election defeat by the English-admired FDR. The reason for the visit was to be an observer for the US which seemed strange to me. The initial reception with Willkie was quite cool until he himself broke the ice. There were press interviews and visits with men and women employed as factory workers, desk clerks, dock workers and employees of various other trades. He talked plain "Hometown USA," laying on the line his real desire for the US to help. As the guest of honor at a monstrous dinner given by Churchill at the Hotel Savoy he was greeted on the way into the event by a group of shouting women, working women, who had been planted in a tea room just outside the banquet hall. "Luk at them capitalistic swine in there swillin' wen we'uns ain't got nottin'," they shouted, along with various other conventional communist slogans. What is OK at Hyde Park Corner doesn't fly at the Hotel Savoy! The girlies got a firm and active heave-ho from the Savoy waiters and porters.

The next day I showed Willkie an intercept from a boot-leg radio sender who was dramatically relaying to the listeners about the brutality shown to the women outside the banquet hall of the Savoy by the waiters and porters. There was mention of all the "swillin' at the Savoy" as well. "At least the girls didn't have to eat the brussels sprouts," commented Willkie, with a big grin on his face. At a later point in time I wrote some speeches for Willkie. Willkie was a pro – he didn't need anyone to write his speeches, he was Willkie!

What, a personal failure? Yes, then came an apparent personal failure. I had to pass the muster with Minister Herschel Johnson who was temporarily in charge until a new ambassador would arrive. General Lee had forgotten to mention this temporary change to me. Johnson thought that my American-type clothes were too much on the "too, too" tight type. So he had Major Sammy Greenwell, a completely "Anglicized" member of the staff, inform me that I was going to get the Savile Row treatment. Being a conformist, I allowed him to drag me down to the partially bombed-out premises of the Huntsmen and Co. shop on Savile Row. In charge was a Mr. Packer, with a most interesting black hairy growth in his ears. The Major explained to him that I would like something to replace my American-type clothes. Packer pulled out a couple of swatches of cloth that he particularly fancied. One was a scrambled egg motif with tomato sauce and verdigris trimming. This cloth was too much, not me. I demanded to see something in a conservative dark blue. They just so happened to have it! I went to the fitting room and found that half of the wall had been blown out, and the thin glass windows were a poor cover against the November cold. The one bright spot in the fitting room was an old picture of Edward as the Prince of Wales.

The vice president in charge of trousers appeared in the room and took approximate lower garment measurements. I admitted that my pants were a trifle tight, but I firmly stipulated that my pants must have some relationship to my body contour, especially since I didn't trust the English braces, or suspenders, which they were called back home. There was the usual reply "Yes. Yes, Sir." along with side remarks such as, "Those Americans! Foreigners!" The pants and vest expert took over calling off a series of numbers to Mr. Packer. Again I stressed, "Not too loose!" and once again there were the usual tolerant smiles. Finally all was finished except for the mere formality of signing the order. The whole job would be "blitzed through," in other words, a rush job, which was going to take about three weeks.

A package was finally delivered to my room at the Claridge, bearing the label Huntsmen and Co., Savile Row. At long last I was to be a properly clad English gentleman! My first try was the trousers. They weren't only loose, they were lewd! During the earlier period of the war it was possible to purchase an occasional grapefruit, so with trousers hoisted to full mast with my braces and pants closely fastened I reached for the grapefruit, tossed it in the air, and with ease slid it through the over ample waistband. That was enough! The suit is going back! Driver Frank and I went to the Huntsmen and

Co. I wore the new suit and had the grapefruit in hand. For the full impact of my complaint, I repeated the same catching trick with the grapefruit I had done earlier. In pleading tones, I spoke of the danger of broken braces with embarrassing exposure and requested closer bodily conformation of the suit. The company agreed to tailor the suit, and the final result was not bad. The pants seat was so ample that I would be standing before the final cloth left the chair. With a blue Eden Homberg hat and a scarf I actually felt OK. Incidentally the entire suit, which included the pants, coat, and vest cost fifteen guineas, or approximately $65.00, and the grapefruit was very expensive as well!

The "guinea" is the non-existent coin with the value of a pound plus a shilling. Real artists, such as lawyers, doctors and hoteliers from the high-class hotels, invariably quote in guineas merely to show that the charge is an approximate one and that there was no real interest in the money. However it should be noted that the value of the guineas fluctuated, but it was always a bit more than the pound, not less. For instance, the charge for my superb room at the Claridge was also rendered in guineas. The charge per day was one guinea. I welcomed the simplicity of the hotel's accounting! The pound rate at the time was equivalent to $4.40 in US dollars, and this was the going rate for the hotel's top floor apartments. It was such a deal because if a bomb should hit the building it would probably hit the top floor first. Prices were in inverse proportion to height. As a mark of special courtesy, I was taken by a member of the Netherlands Court to the third basement floor of the Claridge in the vicinity of the quarters of Queen Wilhelmina. I was there not to intrude on her privacy, but as a music lover I was desirous of hearing a slumber symphony snored in true Wagnerian style! I spent only a month of regal elegance at the Claridge for less than $5.00 a day, then moved to my supposedly permanent quarters.

My new flat at the Landsdowne House was very small and located on the second floor, with a long narrow room leading off to a tiny bedroom, bath, and a somewhat primitive kitchen. It fronted Berkley Square and was only four short blocks from the Embassy. One favorable feature was the one window looking out over the portico entrance which was covered with the very popular "Mamie's Drawers," a lace-like mesh glued to the glass. Should a bomb go off in the vicinity, the "Mamie's Drawers" would supposedly lay the glass down in neat sheets instead of splinters of glass flying about.

The flat was sufficiently furnished, so I immediately made the move to supply the more necessary items, which included cases of Old Panther bourbon. Back in 1917, Saccone and Speed of the S&S Co., established liquor importers, had anticipated the arrival of thirsty bourbon-drinking Americans and had laid in storage tens of thousands of cases of Old Panther bourbon, which had probably been ten years in bond before bottling. To the amazement of Saccone and Speed, the newly overseas Yanks demonstrated a positive taste for Scotch. So the Old Panther bourbon languished for years in the S&S cellars and dock warehouses. During WW2 the docks became a favorite target for the Luftwaffe. It would be a shame if the Luftwaffe bombed the stored Old Panther, as I was interested in purchasing some cases for the apartment. With my diplomatic status, all duties on imported liquors were waived. The price of Old Panther in quarts was approximately $9.00 per case. I had concerns about the storage of these cases at my Landsdowne House flat (which was later bombed) and at a second flat off Hyde Park, which also caught one. My principle difficulty was in finding a temporary resting place and transport for these ten cases of Old Panther along with a few other assorted liquors.

Below the entrance of the Landsdowne House, which was safely guarded by thick pavement, was one of the popular night clubs. It was a must go-to place for everyone until one night when there was a series of big ones dropped. The thick pavement over the night club didn't stop anything! The entire orchestra and eighty guests died that evening. That same evening I was returning home to my flat around midnight and saw ambulances and police all over Berkley square. I passed through all the security lines and went upstairs to my super-safe second story apartment. It was dark and the air seemed a bit cooler than usual, but something I was sensing kept me from turning on the light switch. So I flashed my feeble beamed night lamp instead. There was no blackout curtain over the window. There was no window! The flat had a literal carpet of glass over the floor, my bed and my dresser. That evening bomb number two had landed on the street below my flat, blowing out most of the building's side. That night I slept in the bathtub cushioned by a spare blanket. The following morning I sadly gazed around at what had been my flat. Then my eyes fell on the ten cases of restorative which were untouched! I had piled the cases around the corner from the main room where there was a wall that protected them from the initial blast. I immediately open a bottle, which was cold, room temperature, and took a deep slug. That was one night that I was glad I didn't come home early.

Ambassador John Winant arrived at the Embassy shortly after the bombing of Berkley Square. John was a quiet and modest man. His pants were slightly wrinkled and he had the appearance of Abe Lincoln. Not only did he have the appearance of Lincoln, he had much the feeling of Lincoln. He was craggy-faced, with heavy bushy black hair and deep recessed eyes that gave you the feeling that he was looking inside of you, which he was. John was a man far above politics, dedicated to the idea of everyone being entitled to a run for the money. Towards the end of his ambassadorship (between the years 1944-1945) John was responsible for coordinating and clarifying the Allied Forces on war policy. Considering the different schools of thought and the various plans for division, there was always special emphasis on Berlin. Each nation, at heart, wanted to win the military victory of Berlin and had their individual way of dividing a conquered Germany. Roosevelt had his own plan and, peculiarly enough, kept it a secret from the Allies. Churchill had another plan, and Stalin had not only a different plan but the determination to accomplish his.

I went to visit John Winant in 1944. He spoke of the difficulties in getting any concrete plan from Roosevelt. He would not commit any real backing against other rival plans and demands. I saw John for the last time in Washington D.C. immediately after the war. He was deeply depressed over the bickering between the Allies and the most unsatisfactory solution of the occupation problems. As an idealist, which he was, I think he was frustrated over the final settlement, which probably was the cause of his later suicide.

When Averill Harriman arrived on the scene in London as Defense Expeditor, he dealt directly with FDR. Harriman was very business-like and efficient, using only the Embassy coding facilities. He did a good job not only in London but also in Moscow. Officers and experts began streaming into the already overcrowded No. 1 facility. I was instructed to find other quarters in the vicinity of the Berkley Square. There was No. 20 and No. 18 which were available as office spaces which were located on the opposite corner of the Square. The building had considerable damage from the bombings but had recently been repaired and converted into offices for the newly arriving Special Observers Group under General Andrews of the Air Corps. Unfortunately, General Andrew's plane was hit and went down while on a return trip to the USA.

Adjoining the No. 20 facility was another apartment house, including the luxurious flat of Lady Leslie Doverdale, a socialite whose capital originated from bird deposits found on some of the southern islands. Leslie was active in every way possible. As a member of the Red Cross she was detailed to drive a doughnut wagon, delivering indigestible goods to workers on the docks. Oftentimes Lady Doverdale would forget to close the rear door of the truck, spilling doughnuts along the streets from Buckingham Palace, where the truck was loaded, to the local shipping dock which was the point of delivery. Perhaps the spilling of doughnuts along the way was a blessing in disguise: the life expectancy of the dock workers was probably prolonged!

Lady Doverdale was an extraordinary hostess. Quite often her flat was the scene of brilliant parties. One particular evening her guest list included Roosevelt's emissary, a dreamy but very dedicated Harry Hopkins. Harry was quiet and effaceable and seemed out of place under these war conditions. He never appeared to mingle with his colleagues or the British at the party. When he was asked to be the judge in a bitter argument between the hostess and two lady guests as to who had put out the most firebombs in the light raid that had occurred earlier in the evening, he was unwilling to be a part of it. As for the fact that there had been only two bombs which were dropped that evening and three claimants demanding glory for putting the firebombs out, Harry got his hat and departed for his hotel, thinking that it was probably quieter in Moscow than at the party.

There was another incident that same evening. Among the guests was an Australian journalist, Ward Price, whose popularity among both fellow journalists and locals was at an all-time low. Towards the end of the evening Ward had become obnoxiously overloaded with booze and was feeling a sudden urge to use the boudoir. Lady Doverdale's apartment had the ultimate in everything including her intimate plumbing. The bidet had more controls than an aircraft panel, with various pedals designed to give swirls, flushes and jet propulsion. Dashing for the hostess' boudoir he disposed of his problem in the bidet. While still leaning over the bidet he inadvertently pressed the super jet propulsion pedal. He was totally caught by surprise; it couldn't have happened to a more deserving person.

The first VIP I encountered while in London was Congressman J. Buell Snyder of Pennsylvania, who was equipped with just about everything, including a personal letter from FDR. Snyder had a deep resonant voice and the perfect congressional approach. He held my shoulder with his left hand and clasped firmly my right hand with his right hand, making sure to look directly into my eyes. He said to me, "I'm Snyder of Pennsylvania. Tell me your name son, so I can write your mother and tell her what a good job you are doing." Billy

Rootes of Rootes Motors organized a small motor caravan for the congressman. There were British and US flags flying from each car and motorcycle escort as we passed through each borough. It wasn't difficult to steer him away from Dover, but a visit to Coventry, which had recently been obliterated, was a must.

En route to Coventry we made a brief stop in the town of Rugby in order to inspect the bronze tablets listing the fallen soldiers of WWI. While looking over the names on the tablets I noticed several last names with Chrystal but no McChrystals. Could it be possible that some ancestral stalwarts, facing difficulties in those early days, could have made their way over to Ireland and for convenience sake placed a "Mc" in front of Chrystal? I guess it could be possible. Seeing as there was no constituent material we decided to be on our way to Coventry. Upon our arrival to Coventry we saw that the entire center of the town was a mass of brick and rubble except for the City Hall, a red-stoned architectural monstrosity that would make any architectural designer weep. It had been partially destroyed but was still standing and functional. Possibly the German pilot felt that he had punished the town enough and let the building stand.

The entrance to the City Hall was lined on both sides with members of the Homeguard equipped with various types of rifles and all saluting in an irregular fashion. At the doorway stood the Mayor of the town with a chain and insignia of his office draped across his ample paunch. There were mutual salutes and introductions made before we were escorted to the Mayor's chambers, where there was a very tasty sherry waiting for us as a welcoming gift. We toasted to the King of England and the President of the United States and then the Mayor started in on a flowery speech of welcome and expressed his thanks for the assistance being rendered by the USA. I could see a gleam in Congressman Snyder's eye as he noticed several note takers. The Mayor ended his speech amid applause and shouts of "Hear, Hear!"

Snyder, in his best congressional tones, began to speak: "Mr. Mayor, it is a rare privilege for me as a member of the law making body of the United States, and to see with my own eyes that spirit, that will, that determination to carry on and all that we have epitomized in the English language as Coventry! Mr. Mayor, I subscribe one hundred percent! Mark you, one hundred percent! To those immortal words of Winston Churchill, 'There'll always be an England!' I thank you."

A short time later I quietly suggested to Congressman Snyder that while I was not sure who wrote those immortal words he spoke I would bet money that it wasn't Churchill. Responding to my comment, the Congressman blandly remarked, "What immortal words?"

It was around noon time now and lunch was served to all the guests. After lunch we visited the ruins of the Coventry Cathedral where we viewed a burnt wooden cross marking the tabernacle. As we posed for the customary press photographs our Congressman stated, "In this spot hallowed by sacrifice we should stand with our hats held over our left breasts." This ensuing picture reminded me of an Undertakers convention.

The Coventry trip was not the only scheduled event for the congressman. Snyder had made a special request to meet Raczynski, the Prime Minister of Poland. There was no problem making the arrangements for this meeting, because Tony Biddle, then the Ambassador to the nine countries in exile, was available and willing to set up the meeting right away. The meeting was most successful and I was grateful for the fact that there were no glitches to deal with that night.

Later that evening I decided to take a series of press pictures of the event, which I brought to the doughty legislator while resting up in the Claridge's Hotel. He was munching on a watercress sandwich when I arrived. The sandwich was much easier on his stomach than all the rich foods he had been eating for days. I showed the blown-up prints to him: there was a picture showing the Congressman grasping

Prime Minister Raczynski by the hand, another with his hand on the ambassadorial shoulder, and a third picture where he is practically embracing the diplomat. "Young fellow, I want to thank you for these pictures. Do you have any idea what these will mean when I get back to my Polish constituency in Scranton, Pennsylvania?"

Snyder was just one of the seemingly unending streams of visitors I spent time with. Some of the visitors were serious and some were phony but they all were interesting in their own way. My handling routines would vary depending on the individual: the personal treatment varied from the "Keys of the City" to blue plate specials, and not all the visitors got to stay at the Claridge's Hotel.

Where there were houses or flats that remained unbombed, one would see feeble attempts in the construction of individual family shelters. Those residing in these dwellings were certain that the shelters would be able to withstand a near miss of a bomb, but that was debatable. The following and much commented on advertisement appeared in the *Daily Telegraph:*

HOME AIR-RAID SHELTERS

EASILY BUILT

EVERY SIZE

SLEEPING TWO UPWARDS

The only real protection against heavy bombs was afforded by underground bank vaults, ten-story deep War Rooms such as those belonging to the Bank of England where treasure depositories were stored. Among the so-called safer spots was the residence of Ambassador Kennedy, with his private concrete and steel underground shelter. This shelter was subject to some comment, especially since his successor, John Winant and wife, lived in a normal steel-brick apartment house adjoining the Embassy at No. 1 Grosvenor Square. Kennedy's apparent feeling that England had little if any chance against the Germans was a cause for bitter comments among many of the British. The British were especially bitter towards Kennedy, hearing that when he had returned to the USA in October 1940 he gave several speeches, in which, according to a commentator, Kennedy had advised giving all kinds of assistance to England, short of help! Lord Halifax was especially outspoken about Kennedy.

Social life was rather on the quiet side during the heavy bombing periods. This was especially true of the larger gatherings in the various cafes and night clubs, which, under pre-war conditions were often located in basements or under paved entryways of various hotels. The time when the night club, which was located in the basement of my apartment in the Landsdowne House, was bombed, killing 80 people, was the point when restrictions were made on large gatherings. People were worried, very worried. Private get-togethers at various flats and houses became more and more popular; they were usually held on the progressive system which basically meant from house to house. The smart move was to have the last get-together on ones' home grounds, which obviated the difficult task of getting a taxi late at night or being subjected to the various hazards of walking home in the black of the blackouts. The blackout hazards were neither thieves nor robbers but were the various missing guardrails or courtyards which sat below sidewalk level. The most dangerous night-time hazards were the solid, unlit and just below the waist-high sidewalk collection boxes of the British Post.

My Embassy position brought me into close contact with members of the press, both American and English. These correspondents were very professional, not recent graduates from a journalism school like those we see today who seem to play such an active role in reporting world events. Among my press contacts were Ed Mowrer, Bill Stoneman, Helen Kirkpatrick, Jim Reston, Drew Middleton, and Mary Welsh Monks, who later became Mary Hemingway. These were only a few of the press covering the British scene during my stay, and working with them as well as various broadcasting groups enabled me to keep up with home-side events as well as overseas developments.

There was a question as to the advisability of General Raymond Lee making the trip to the USA from London at this particular time, and his plans to travel were taken up twice with the War Department. Twice he was told, "No Danger! Come ahead!" We had received some very hard information at the Embassy from the British as to the danger of a Japanese attack. Lee departed for the USA December 2nd 1941. He arrived by plane to Lisbon then caught a boat from Lisbon to New York. It was on Sunday, December 7th, a clear but bitter cold day, and Lee was expected to be arriving home soon. I checked in at the Embassy briefly and found that Mr. Winant was at Chequers for the weekend with the Prime Minister and General Ralph Royce from the Air Force, who was the acting Attaché and was recently in Scotland looking over possible air-fields.

Since everything seemed to be quiet at the Embassy I got the official car driver, Frank, picked up Jack Coffey and Ralph Snavely, who were from the Special Observer Group, and headed for Sandy Lodge for a game of golf and a relaxing outing in the country. My game from the first tee on turned out to be a catastrophe. I had exceeded my life's worst efforts. From the fairway to rough and still in the rough I found myself shivering in the keen wind, looking for lost balls from normally easy chip shots which flew off in all directions. My only consolation was that the game came to an end and it would be my last round of golf for the winter. The three of us decided to stop off at the club's bar for hot rum, sandwiches of queer spam-like material on dry bread and a spot of conventional tea before we headed back to London. On the way home the car stuttered a few times, which was probably from the usual low-octane gas pains. Overhead were two flights of our bombers, one of twelve and the other of seven. There was a single old De Havilland plane that seemed to be flying sideways in the wind.

Frank dropped off Jack and Ralph at the Dorchester then left me at my flat. For me it was time for hot rum, crackers, a cozy bed and Shirer's book, *Berlin Diary*. Twice in the night I heard the telephone ring but I was too tired to answer it.

That next morning Big Ben bonged at nine o'clock and I tuned in the BBC on the radio for the news. The opening words of the nine o'clock news chased away all ideas of sleep or fatigue. It was unbelievable! The Japanese had bombed Pearl Harbor!!! I immediately thought of Lee: his trip just so happened to coincide with the timing of the bombing of Pearl Harbor. Lee never did return to London. I snatched a heavy coat and my steel helmet and hot-footed it to the Embassy. Within minutes Raymond W. Bliss, Jacob Beam and Dorsey Fisher had arrived at the Embassy simultaneously. I phoned Winant and learned that he was already on his way back to London. We worked on getting everything set at the Embassy between news flashes. The RAF was to inform General Royce in Scotland of the situation. I phoned General Chaney and Colonel McClelland of the Special Observer Group and told them of the situation and to stand by. Colonel Van Voorst of the Signal Corp was to set up a continuous cable and code watch.

News flashes, news intercepts, press reports and inquiries kept coming in: "Pearl Harbor raided again with ninety planes!" "Roosevelt orders Army/Navy to engage in previously prepared battle plan,!" then a press side query, "What have they been doing?" More news flashes: "Attacks on Honolulu are heavy and continuous"; "American Battleship sunk at mooring, 350 enlisted men killed, one bomb, Hickham Field. Terrific loss of life in Honolulu!" The press waited on word from Churchill relative to his pledge to declare war within the hour if America was attacked. I received a call from Ed Beatty of the United Press reminding me that I had bet a pound with him at Biddle's cocktail party a week earlier that the Japs would not make their move by 8:15 p.m. GMT next Wednesday.

11:10 p.m. – "FDR has called party and cabinet leaders into conference."

11:24 p.m. – "Japan declares war on US and Britain … USS Oklahoma on fire at Pearl … Airfields damaged, preventing take-offs."

11:30 p.m. – Eric Baume, Australian journalist, called and asked what our plans were. I told him we were Australia-bound.

12:00 noon – Call from Charlie Bolte, Special Observer, meeting at 2 Grosvenor, all in uniform, in accordance with instructions from Secretary of War, Stimpson. Unconfirmed press report: "We had gotten Jap aircraft carrier." "Japs attack Malaya." Word was received that Churchill was convening House at 3:00 p.m., Monday, December 8th.

In the meantime the Embassy vicinity became very crowded and it became necessary to order police detail and Marine Guard to take position at the entrance. It was December 8th, 1941, around 1 o'clock in the morning when "Putt" Turner, acting Air Force Attaché, came to the Embassy with a half pheasant, a can of corn on the cob and a bottle of Old Pioneer for our late night dinner. We cooked the pheasant and corn on a sterno cooker. While cooking, Ambassador Winant arrived, bringing his lunch which had been thoughtfully prepared by Churchill's staff. This was a welcome addition to the menu. Winant was given the run-down of the situation over dinner.

4:30 a.m. – Crashing sound in room adjoining the office. Expecting Jap spies but discovered that it was several mice upsetting dinner dishes. In the meantime Winant had gone to his flat along with Turner. I left instructions at the Embassy to call and keep calling me until I pick up should there be any updates and hit it for my humble pad at No. 3.

9:00 a.m. – Arrived at the Embassy in uniform. The uniformed Marine Guard at the entrance saluted me smartly. I had a feeling of relief. The situation was tragic but it had happened in a manner that would give unity to America and commensurate strength.

10:00 a.m. – General Royce returns to the Embassy to confirm my orders for a complete stand-by. Jacobs phoned in, saying that he could get six airplane tickets for the House [the Embassy]. Incoming cables for the day were two instead of hundreds. Changes were made to some of the officers' status. For the first time we were dealing with the "Forgotten Front" – Hawaii! Mary Welsh from *Time Magazine* called in for the color of the story; red-faced was all that I could suggest. Further queries came into the Embassy; questions as to where the reconnaissance was taking place. Reports were made about the loss of three battleships, three destroyers and the loss of 15,000 lives.

2:00 p.m. – Started out for the House of Commons with the Embassy party. Winant went ahead of us. Photographers were everywhere! Inside the rotunda were hundreds of people milling around waiting for the members of the House to come in. The meeting was in the cushioned House of Lords because the House of Parliament was still under repair from a previous bombing. When the Speaker of the House entered the rotunda we were able to go inside.

It was 3:00 p.m. by the time the procession started from the Members Anteroom into the House of Lords as the police loudly called out, "Strangers, take off your hats!" Leading the procession was the Bearer of the Mace, then the Speaker of the House, in a robe with a long grey wig. Following were three clerks and the Chaplain. We were ushered to the Distinguished Strangers Gallery which seated about a dozen people. In the Ambassadors' Gallery across the way was Wellington Koo of China, Cartier of France, Raczynski of Poland, our John Winant of the US, and others. After the Speaker entered, Churchill and Mrs. Churchill entered the Gallery, walking through the crowd below. Mrs. Churchill later joined John Cowdray in the Gallery. From one of the benches below came a wave from Nancy Astor, an American-born Member of Parliament.

The crowd hushed as Churchill moved to the Dispatch Box and began to speak. His voice was firm yet quiet as he announced that Japan had attacked both America and Great Britain. He stated that he had spoken with Roosevelt earlier in the evening last night and that the American Congress would be meeting at 12:00 noon in Washington. Due to the time lapse between Great Britain and America he was not going to wait to declare war. Churchill stated, "Great Britain has also been attacked!" as he punctuated his address – "Hear, hear!" He continued with a firm voice and without any evident emotion. During his speech a slip of paper was handed to him; he merely glanced at it then continued speaking. As he finished his address the speakers from the Opposition, the Labor and Socialist parties, showed their full support of his action, and then followed Secretary of State for War, Leslie Hore-Belisha, who spoke at length in support of the Prime Minister. During his remarks he referred to all the nations engaged except for one, China. A chorus of voices corrected him and into the box came that same slip of paper that had been handed to Churchill. China had been forgotten!

As the House adjourned we moved out to the rotunda. Mary Welsh, of *Time Magazine,* introduced me to Roland Tree of the English Press's fame and power. Slightly to my embarrassment, he asked me if I had just arrived. I then had the opportunity to shake hands with Churchill, which made me feel better. He asked me what I thought of his Declaration. Charles Turner and Pugge, MPs, invited us to the Members' Lounge for a drink. I returned to the Embassy around 4:30 p.m. and then went to my flat at #3 Grosvenor Square. General Royce and Bob McClure stopped by, so I issued an informal dinner invitation to them along with Helen Kirkpatrick and Joe Evans, whom I had seen earlier at the Embassy. Everyone had arrived by 6:00 p.m., in time to watch Roosevelt's address to Congress asking for a Declaration of War. He spoke for about six minutes. The applause greeting seemed a little canned, but as he finished there was no question about the applause: we were together, united at last! Paul

Robeson's song, something about peace, began to air and it was so out of place we cut the broadcast.

Royce left after the broadcast and I started the preparations for an "Ambassadorial Dinner," with Hormel ham, onion soup and corn on the cob, which was canned as usual. I called in a near-by waiter to assist. Everything was going fine until my fuse burnt out on my two-plate burner. Dinner was served semi-warm along with many bottles of 1928 vintage wine. Winant seemed tired and as we toasted to America, and FDR. He took me aside and told me of the foul-up in the arrangements between FDR and Churchill which often left him without any real direction. At 9:00 p.m. we listened to the BBC to hear Churchill repeating his address in the House. I had never listened to him speak when he sounded so tired and spiritless. I must admit that at this point I felt frayed myself.

All day long on December 9th the Embassy was jammed with people. There were Americans who wanted to enlist or get back their lapsed commissions. There were those who wanted to transfer from the English or Canadian forces to the US forces. There was no draft card burning that day!

A real VIP visitation was the arrival of the first contingent of US troops, the 34th Division, who first landed in Belfast, Ireland, under the command of Major General "Scrappy" Hartle. This was the first opportunity for the newly formed US Press Service group from G-2 to function under actual wartime conditions. The security was excellent upon the troops' arrival as they disembarked from laden transports and assembled on the long quay to be addressed by the Lord Governor of Northern Ireland. Due to static imperfections of the loud-speaker system and the English accent of Lord Governor, the troops didn't know if they were being greeted in Swahili or Arabic. It was only after they started marching to their billets among the crowds of cheering Irish did they realize that they were on the Old Sod. One of the most repeated comments of the various spectators was, "Look at the boots on the boys, sure an' they bend!" The entire press contingent was on hand from London and the security was so tight that it was difficult to get any news. Dave Duncan, a top photographer, entrusted me with his Leica camera, seeing as I could get on board. The net result of my picture-taking was one great shot and two pictures of my thumb.

At dinner that evening Dave and I did bootlegging with Bill Darby, of later Darby Ranger fame. Bill was very influential, and as a guest that night he was able to provide a chunk of steak with an egg! Shades of Lucullus! [an Optimate politician of the late Roman republic] The press office of the Special Observer Group informed us that they had definitely made the arrangements that the story would be held until the following day at noon to give the weeklies and magazines an even break with reporters actually being on the scene. Both FDR and Churchill had apparently been muzzled. At peace with the world, several members of the press, including Larry Rue of the *Chicago Tribune,* went aboard the ferry steamer headed for Liverpool, which was due to leave at 9 o'clock in the morning. As the mooring lines were being loosened, the 9 o'clock BBC news announced, "The American Troops have landed in Northern Ireland!" A couple of the reporters who were close to the rail of the steamer sprang to the dock. The reporters hadn't filed their copy of the news because, under agreement, nothing was to be released until noon the following day.

Poor Larry Rue was below deck having a refreshing beer as the BBC blared out the announcement. It was too late for him to spring ashore. Larry tore at his sparse locks as he yelled out, "I'm ruined professionally! Ruined!" Striding up and down the deck he drank beer after beer, and in no time the beer supply was gone, but not Larry's dejection. It just so happened that Helen Kirkpatrick of the rival *Chicago News,* knowing that Larry hadn't filed a copy of the news, shot a short take to the London Bureau under Rue's name. As to a break of the agreement concerning the timed release of the news it just so happened that the new Press setup had made an error: they had blocked off FDR and Churchill but forgot to block off Secretary Stimpson.

Another visitor of prominence was a modest little Archbishop, Francis Spellman. Cardinal Arthur Hinsley, who was the ranking Catholic prelate in England, had just died and his funeral plans were underway. Archbishop Spellman was in Gibraltar en route to the Middle-East when he was directed to attend Hinsley's funeral in London. Airspace was limited in those days and the only transportation that was available to him was space in the cargo hold of the RAF mail plane. Two bags of mail were unloaded from the plane in order to make room for the Archbishop. He was pushed inside the plane among all the mail bags and then, "Tally Ho for Dear Old England!"

There was a bit of competition for the visitor upon his arrival at the Euston station. The British had sent a staff car with a WAF driver, the Papal Nuncio sent another car, and I was ordered by Winant to look for him. After battling my way through eager reporters at the station I found the Archbishop, who was exhausted after his six-hour ride in the cockpit of the mail plane. I grabbed him, hustled him past the waiting press, and pushed him into the nearest car, which was the British Embassy auto. The girl driver was so impressed and excited that she immediately took off and by accident hit a fire hydrant, blowing a front tire. The cleric and I jumped out of the car and ran over to where my car was parked. I opened the car door and put the Archbishop in with my driver, Claridge's. When all was clear I loudly ordered him to take the cleric to the Papal Nuncio. The following morning the Archbishop, still a little dazed, came to visit the Embassy and Mr. Winant. His one question and hope was that he hadn't hurt anyone's feelings.

After the impressive ceremony of Cardinal Hinsley's funeral, the Archbishop decided to change his travel plans and go to Ireland for a short visit. I was detailed as his political advisor. This man needed political advice like he needed two left feet! Due to political complications, Spellman refused the offer of an RAF plane and rented a small two-motor job for the crossing into Dublin. Flying from Liverpool to Dublin can be rough, and this flight was no exception. I was only glad that if we dunked into the water I would be in good company.

Upon our arrival at Dublin's Collinstown airport we were met by the Irish press and public officials, including Ambassador David Grey of the USA. Spellman and I had a quick huddle over the churchly remarks that had been made and his solution was, "I'll tell them that I'm glad to be back where me mother and father were born!" This I instantly approved of. He went on to say, "Besides, that will be the first time they ever got their names in the paper."

It was three busy days of meetings, conferences, and dinners with the Princes of the Church, the Canadian Commissioner Kearney, the UK Representative, John Maffey, and naturally, the Prime Minister, Devalera. Crowds followed the Archbishop in Dublin, often shouting out, "Save us from the bombs!" and "God Bless America!" For three successive evenings we listened to Minister Devalera's long and moody recitals of his hardships while he was escaping from England. He had to hide under a tarpaulin while rats ate his sandwiches and chewed on his raincoat. His often-repeated statement was that he had visited every one of the forty-eight states and knew, beyond a doubt, that America sympathized with and approved of the Irish neutrality stand. It was the combination of Bushmill and boredom after having to listen to so much repetition by the Minister that led me to venture the opinion that, while his wide US travels were fully admitted, he could have stayed in Boston, as his only contacts were the usual groups of Irish Micks shouting, "Up Dev!" And "I am a Mick!" The Archbishop closed the affair that evening with a toast "To the President of the United States and the principles for which he stands!"

The second phase of the churchly Irish tour was complicated. It involved a quick visit to the Cardinal of Armagh in the North, who actively disliked anything American. Our auto trip from Dublin to Armagh was basically uneventful except for running off the main road. When I asked directions from an old Irish biddy, there was a twinkle in her eye as she asked, "Are ye's on the nod?" In other words, were we making an illegal border crossing. When I told her who my companion was she made the sign of the cross and eagerly indicated the correct road. We arrived at the Cardinal's residence before noon and I decided to visit the nearby pub for a shot of restorative and then wait outside until 1:30 p.m., which was our scheduled time to leave Armagh and head for Belfast, where we would make a quick visit to the American troops.

Within minutes of waiting outside the Cardinal's residence, David Gray reappeared and as he got into his car he wished me well. I was then informed that the Cardinal, despite our schedule, had planned on starting lunch at 1:30 p.m. Once again, trusting the Bushmill, which was one of the basic causes of the Irish civil wars, I sent for the Cardinal's houseman and bluntly informed him that the lunch schedule had better be speeded up and that the Archbishop would be called for at 1:30 p.m.! I decided to go back to the pub for a sandwich and another restorative.

At 1:30 p.m. I re-entered the residence of the Cardinal, moving into the spacious dining-room. I bowed reverently to the Cardinal and informed Archbishop Spellman that departure time had arrived. It was obvious that the luncheon had been speeded up as per my request, seeing as the coffee and liqueurs were on the table. The Cardinal seemed less forbidding than reputed as he shouted, "It's a tyrant you are! You'd let him stay three days down below and you begrudge him two hours here!" Perhaps it was providence or something else that prompted my reply, "Your Eminence, ten minutes with you is worth two weeks with those saplings in Dublin!" With a half-smile the Cardinal beckoned me, "Kneel down you rogue! I'll bless you, and you sure need it!" I got his blessing, kissed his ring, and then grabbed Spellman and his coat, and off we went on our way to Belfast.

Once in Belfast we had a short talk with the Lord Governor of North Ireland and a quick meeting with Colonel Hill and the US Airmen stationed nearby. Before long we were on the night boat to Liverpool, on schedule and on protocol.

This visit to Ireland with Spellman was not free from diplomatic boots on my part. Before I departed to Ireland I was briefed by the Embassy as to various personalities that I may encounter. I had been told that President Hyde had been a professor at Columbia University, however they forgot to mention that it was in 1905. Colonel Vansetti of the Chemical Warfare Service happened to be on leave from Columbia and was currently at the Embassy in London, so in my official call to the President, while in Ireland, I thought it would be proper to bring imaginary regards from his old colleague of Columbia, which brought tears and pleasure to the aging old man. I relayed to David Grey my conversation that I had with the President and it was he who informed me as to the period Hyde was at Columbia. David invited me to his residence, and upon my arrival with champagne in hand a call came in from the Irish press. The press inquired if the Colonel Vansetti that had sent his greetings to President Hyde had any relation to the Sacco-Vansetti bomb murders.

There was a two-year period during which I flew across the Atlantic many times as a courier bearing dispatches or plans. This was particularly pleasant when one's duty consisted of safe-guarding an important small packet or briefcase for the cause. However, later on this duty became somewhat less desirable when the contents of the so-called diplomatic pouch consisted of a few rolls of a new type of camouflage or a heavy casting of a new motor design or something of that ilk.

Originally the routes I took were simple – I would board a BOAC flight to Lisbon then catch the Pan-Am Clipper (flying boat) via Azores to Bermuda and then on to New York. This route changed for me because of the possible French interference. The flights on the flying boats would veer wide over the ocean outside of Dakar to Balama in Portugese New Guinea and from that point would head to either Belem or Trinidad before landing in New York.

Eventually, travelling on a clipper was abandoned because they were too slow. So the Ferry Command route over the North Atlantic became the standard run. Now I would fly from London to Shannon, then to Reykjavik, then to either Goose Bay or Gander before landing in New York. My top ride for a straight endurance flight was when I flew from Prestwick, Scotland in a B-26 bomber which had been converted to passenger use by putting eight seats behind the cockpit. However there was no heating. The seven passengers and I were dressed for the Arctic with fur parkas, trousers, boots and fur hoods and we all sat like stuffed mummies, four on each side. When it came to personal requirements, it meant a walk on a narrow plank just beyond the door opening to do the "bomb-bay" and that was to be done only once per passenger.

It was solid fog when we left Prestwick, there was fog over Iceland, and no visibility over Goose Bay or Gander. This made landing almost impossible. Finally we received news that the sky was fairly open above Montreal and we landed after a sixteen -hour direct flight with only a small gas load left. Needless to say, the other passengers and I developed an aversion to air-flight that lasted until we got a decent night's sleep.

That next morning we boarded the plane and continued on to New York and Washington D.C. One of the passengers on the flight was the Duke of Hamilton, with whom I had an interesting conversation about Rudolf Hess, one of Hitler's deputies in the Nazi party. Being interested in various youth movements, Hamilton had met Hess on the continent a few years prior and found him extremely able and well-informed, especially in the youth field. Hess, using the name Alfred Horn, had asked to see the Duke, among other requests, after he had made a bad parachute landing and broke his leg. It is possible that he had in mind some kind of deal that he wanted to discuss with the Duke based on an appeal for youth on both sides. He had spent nearly the entire day trying to explain to the various Home Guards just exactly who he was but they couldn't care less. The Duke eventually spoke with him. Years later Hess ended up in confinement in the Spandau Prison being found guilty of crimes against peace and crimes against humanity in 1946, a most unreasonable situation since he ended up being the last and only prisoner, an infirm and a broken old man. A hospital bed and a guard would have sufficed.

On one of my flying boat trips we flew past Dakar to Bolama Bay, which was on the coast of Portuguese New Guinea. I discovered the inefficiency of sign language as a means of communication on this trip. Our clipper landed at dawn on Bolama Bay. In the town of Bolama were several stone buildings, the Governor's house, a Customs shed and various warehouses. It seemed that all the other structures in town were thatched huts. Crowds of natives gathered around to see the "Big Flying Bird" with much intrigue. There were fish jumping all over the bay and I, being a keen fisherman, immediately wanted fishing tackle. With my vague memory of the Latin language I asked for "linha de pesca" (fish line), which secured me a rope heavy enough to catch a whale. Now I needed fish hooks, but asking for fish hooks in Portuguese or the native tongue seemed to be a real problem. So I opted to make various gestures in order to get my point across. I made a gesture of a fisherman dragging his catch out of the water with bent fingers at the end of an imaginary rope which left the populace wondering what I was doing. At this point I was frustrated, so I tried another gesture, which was to put my bent finger in my mouth to convey the fishhook idea. This didn't work either. The local people continued to stare at me in wonderment.

It wasn't until 5 o'clock in the afternoon when the flying boat was being readied for take-off that I saw some of the locals approach me. I heard loud shouts from the village, then a long procession of villagers headed by their chief neared the Customs shed where I was standing. The group halted and the chief himself approached me with a wide grin and proudly presented me with an old set of false teeth. I registered joy and thankfulness for the gift and in return I scattered small coins among the crowd. We prepared for take-off in the flying boat headed for England eventually, and as I gazed out the window, fish were still jumping freely in Bolama Bay.

It was now the middle of February 1942, and a number of officers were arriving at the Embassy for inspections as well as to consult with planning groups. Lieutenant General John Clifford Hodges Lee, nicknamed "General Jesus Christ Himself Lee" and "General John Court House Lee" arrived with a colored driver, white gloves and a Cadillac that was so long that it could have blocked two tiny London streets with ease. General Lee was slated to handle the supplies for the U.S. Forces as well as the judicial court system. General McNarnay returned back to London after taking part in the Pearl Harbor commission, which was called the Robert's Commission. With all the various visitors showing up, the flats in Grosvenor Square were being taken over. The Norfolk House had been leased, which served as the planning headquarters for the projected North Africa Invasion. Ambassador Tony Biddle had secured an entire building to house his various guests and their activities for the nine countries in exile. One of his guests was His Royal Majesty, King Peter of Yugoslavia, whose rule lasted exactly eight days. The King was provided a desk and various amenities. There were definitely signs of stress all around. Power group buildups among various blocs developed along with minor jealousies, but this all seemed to diminish when Eisenhower arrived to start the planning of "Torch."

From Washington came word that General Raymond Lee, whose arrival to the U.S. from London coincided with the Japanese attack on Pearl Harbor, had taken over Military Intelligence, replacing General Miles. Lee's new position was an ideal choice for the military to make because Lee had years of diplomatic experience and familiarity with British staffs and methods. I became troubled when I received a long garbled cable from Lee directing me to close out my affairs as quickly as possible and report to him in Washington. It didn't take me long to make arrangements for my departure. I made plans with "Putt" Turner to divide my supply of Old Pioneer as well as a few other items among those interested. I made the same arrangements with General Lee's restorative supply.

Before my departure I held a dinner party for various guests, which included Ambassador Winant and his wife, "Putt" Turner, and Lady Astor. A certain feature that evening, or should I say a request, was that upon the guests' departure I asked if they would please take a number of rolls of the softest tissue, naturally unwrapped. It was the expression of true appreciation that the Mistress of Cliveden, Lady Astor, walked out of #3 Grosvenor Square with several rolls of the finest soft tissue slung over her shoulder. I bid my fellow colleagues a farewell and was off to Washington to see General Lee.

I reported to General Lee directly upon my arrival. When I saw him I was shocked. He had a tense, drawn face and trembling fingers. In the privacy of his office he slowly informed me that his nerves could just not take it anymore, especially since he felt strained with the responsibility for all the Army Intelligence. There had been a minor feud in England with McNarney. A second feud had flared up again over the Pearl Harbor Investigation findings in which McNarney had participated. The sum of Lee's stress was the three solid years of strain and the bombing of London. I joked with him, then I swore at him to get some kind of reaction from him but it was to no avail. Lee felt incapable of doing the type of job required. I left his office and went directly to see Major General George V. Strong, who had recently been assigned Assistant G-2. I told him of the strains that Lee had been under, with all the bombings and the wheeling and dealing with top political personages of various nations. He had driven himself mercilessly, he was a physical wreck! I suggested to Strong that Lee be given at least a month leave or more in order to enable him to get his nerves back in shape. Lee was given leave but after six weeks had passed, General Strong was appointed G-2 and General Lee was put in charge of an Artillery Division.

Before too long I was appointed to work for General Strong, and in turn I worked on him to give me orders back to the war zone. He nicely offered me a position that would eventually bring me a Brigadier General's rating. When I insisted upon going back to the war zone, he decided to send me to the West Coast, where I could work on getting back to the war. In two weeks I was ordered to report to Brigadier General Gilbraith, ex-cavalry, who was now the Commanding General for the San Francisco Port of Embarkation where the military was slowly preparing to serve the entire Pacific. I sent a personal cable to Colonel John Dahlquist, G-1 personnel, in London asking for his assistance to move along my orders to get back to the war.

After my experience in England and now being out of the war zone, it all seemed like child's play to me. It was like children playing war games with mock air-raid alerts for mock raids. What frightened the West Coast residents were either a large whale or a Japanese submarine. I understood the terrific organizational challenges of the S.F. Port; however, for myself I could envision the pending landings in Europe or Africa. At last my welcomed orders came in: Lt. Colonel McChrystal was to proceed to London by the first available transportation for his duty with the American Embassy. In a week I was flying eastward to Washington D.C., New York, Prestwick, and then finally arriving in London.

It was an entirely different picture in London since I was last there last. There was an enormous increase of officers and enlisted staff. Practically every building that surrounded Grosvenor Square was taken except for the Japanese Embassy, which was one block away from the Square. That building was occupied by the Japanese staff under the guard of Scotland Yard.

Because of the tremendous presence of military personnel on the Embassy grounds, per a diplomatic courtesy evolved as an old custom, each Military Attaché would contribute a fixed sum of money per month to be administered by the Secretary of the Association. At this particular point in time it was me. When a Military Attaché was relieved of his duty and left London, he would receive a silver cigarette box which was paid for out of this fund. On the top of the box were the engraved signatures of his colleagues. After the Pearl Harbor attack I questioned the gift of the cigarette boxes to the three Japanese Attachés. When I inquired to the Doyen, Kalla of Czechoslovakia, as to the connection of the six former colleagues to the Military Attachés of the Rising Sun, his face stiffened as he remarked, "We must do the protocol!" When the cigarette boxes arrived I called the Japanese Embassy to let them know that I would be presenting them to the three Military Attachés and that I would be escorted by the convoy of the Senior Scotland Yard Inspector. The inscription on the boxes merely read, "To Lt. Colonel XXX, from your colleagues, London, England," along with the dates of their service. I formally presented the boxes to the Senior Attaché. He greeted me with a "Good morning," took the boxes, bowed and then said, "Goodbye." What? No salutes?

Another duty that I had since my return to London, together with Colonel VanVoorst, was the coding of Churchill's messages to Roosevelt. The message contents were often world-shaking and occasionally very human. The coded messages from Churchill were sent through the Army code machines by a former Navy personnel and the reply from Roosevelt would come through the Navy code system. Perfect cooperation was a requirement and perfect cooperation was given. I recall one particularly vital message that had come in one day from Churchill, and then late that evening another message came in from him by courier from 10 Downing St. in London. Churchill had no conventional cabelese – he merely cabled as he spoke. The second message dealt with a personal problem. He wanted to give

MacArthur a "K.C.B." (Knight Commander of the Bath), but if he did he would have to give one to "Monty" (General Montgomery), and by doing that he felt the gesture would be considered a baby. Roosevelt's reply came in that next day to the Prime Minister and when decoded it roughly said, "It's a wet one and right in your lap."

The power and prestige of the Attachés offices at the Embassy began to materially diminish with all the additional arrivals of special groups, the so called specialists. There were no steps taken to send a replacement for General Lee, so his job fell into the hands of a Senior Officer. I had no other choice but to get used to the inevitable changes at the Embassy.

The military social life kept things interesting. There was a major social event that occurred at the Russian Embassy on November 7th in celebration of Red Army Day. Everyone who was anyone was there, with very few exceptions. One notable absentee was General Eisenhower, however, the word got around that he was merely detained temporarily and that he would be attending the event. The host, Russian Ambassador Maisky, introduced the Sharpshooter of the Soviet Union to the guests. The Sharpshooter was a blocky female in full uniform. In attendance at the event were representatives of various countries in exile, headed by the affable and charming Tony Bindle. Prince Bernhard of the Netherlands, tiny King Peter of Yugoslavia, and Benes of Czechoslovakia were there. British, American, and Canadian Senior Service Officers, Lord Mountbatten, Anthony Eden, and even Lloyd George were present. From our American Embassy was Ambassador Winant. One noticeable and nervous guest was General De Gaulle, who strode from room to room only speaking briefly with a few of his friends.

Despite the excellent vodka and the finest caviar, an air of tension filled the Embassy. As I was standing on the grand staircase, overlooking the crowd, I watched various small groups of guests huddling together in deep discussions. I noticed that Eisenhower had not made the reception, and rumor had it that he was already en route to Gibraltar. All of a sudden an old friend approached me: "Art," he casually murmured, "Are the Americans going in tomorrow or the next day?" I hesitated for a moment then said to him, "An Embassy office boy doesn't get in on everything." I knew that the Allies were landing in North Africa the next morning because I already had my orders to go. I also knew that, due to the distrust of the French in Dakar and Casablanca, General De Gaulle had not been informed of the current plans. Everyone knew except Charlie! De Gaulle never forgot or forgave the fact that he was the last to know of the Allies' North Africa landing.

6. Don't Gild the Lily!

In the distant past when wars were popular or semi-pop, or even tolerated…

I write of the years prior to and following Pearl Harbor, which was the first time in history that the great American public was mad as hell and, incidentally, scared. I was a military attaché in London since October 1940 and had the interesting experience of being bombed some five nights a week, with a special performance on nights of a full moon, and on the next day helped in digging out. Quentian Reynolds told the story best in "The Wounded Do Not Cry," published in *Colliers*. But that was someone else's war.

Then came December 7th and Pearl Harbor. I know of the others who greeted the arrival in England and in Ireland of the first elements of the military, naval and air might of the USA and the grief that marked news of sunken ships. I recall the pride over the bold landings of the Allies on the shores of North Africa. Strangely enough, I do not recall hearing of campus gatherings to celebrate the news that inexperienced US forces had been badly mauled by the veteran tankers of Rommel at Kasserine Pass. I do recall favorable reception of the new that these same amateurs together with the 8th Army Desert Rats had finally chased Rommel and his Italian cohorts out of North Africa. As for college professors, in those days the majority were engaged in teaching and broadcasters had not as yet become self-acknowledged military experts and strategists.

It was September 6, 1943 in Algiers. My duty was to control for the Allied Forces in the Mediterranean a hydra-headed monster – World Press that wanted to tell all; censorship that wanted to stop all; and Psychological Warfare, a new branch, unknown and mistrusted, especially by the higher brass.

Everything was going splendidly. The islands of Lampadusa and Panterillia had been taken with rowboats plus bombs. After a month of vicious fighting, the Germans had been driven out of Sicily and the Italians had signed surrender terms.

The next move was to be the landing of the Fifth Army under General Clark on the Italian mainland, the place Salerno, that time early morning September 9. In addition to the actual landing there were secondary considerations: a planned parachute drop on Rome by the 82nd Airborne, with a team from my propaganda division ready to report from Rome, broadcasting the news of the Italian surrender.

Another incident was the landing of General Max Taylor in a submarine near Rome and a quiet trip into the Holy City for a meeting with Graziani, the successor to Mussolini, and giving him a prepared message, telling of the Italian surrender ... the message to be read by Graziani over Radio Rome at 1715 hours, September 8.

To get the maximum impact of the surrender, the Combined. Chiefs of Staff had decided that the surrender news would be held to coincide with the news of the Allies landing on the mainland. This announcement was to be made by General Eisenhower and the officially approved statement was quietly recorded at Ike's office in the St. George Hotel. No problems at all!

If the paratroop drop by the 82nd Airborne was on, BBC would present an interesting discussion on "Rose Culture in South Africa" at 1500 hrs, Sept. 8. If the drop was off, the subject would be "Gold Mining in South Africa."

Everything was keyed to the main announcement ... the recorded speech by Eisenhower ... the Italians had surrendered and the Allies were landing, scheduled for 1800 hrs. Then came trouble. Early on September 8 came word from the Combined

Chiefs that the Ike announcements would be altered by adding three words: "I AM THUS" to "accepting the surrender of the Italian people." A short addition, but the Supreme Commander had already gone from Algiers en route to La Marsa – Sicilian palace headquarters for the high army and navy brass of the impending landings.

For hours, feverish efforts under tight security were made to cut in the three words on a disk … stop the record … three words … start the record, time after time to match the Eisenhower tone and accent. Finally the voice of a young Tesas captain matched the record.

In a moment of generosity I ordered a duplicate disc cut and sent it under guard to the tiny recording and broadcasting room of what was the origin of AFN, then but a short-range sender, a few soldier disc jockeys, a limited musical library, and transmission over telephone lines to stations in Tunis and Sicily plus Algiers. Instructions were given that the disc be played at 1800 hrs, no other information. This timing also coincided nicely with a high level staff dinner being given by Admiral A.B.C. Cunningham at La Marsa.

My main office in the Maison d'Agriculture, Algiers, resembled an armed camp and the center of a major sending and receiving agency: there were security guards on all doors, receivers to monitor BBC and Radio Rome; Pool press stories on fast tape were ready to follow the Eisenhower announcement, plus additional taped individual stories.

All set! 1500 hrs. The BBC announcer spoke of the importance of gold mining in South Africa. No parachute drop!

At 1730 a group of listeners gathered round the monitor desk, ready for the next announcement … Graziani from Rome. Soft Italian music. 1745 hrs … a hush and more soft Italian music. Five minutes passed. Then another five. Then a loud announcement, followed by a droning voice. Comparison with written text showed Graziani was finally on the air.

1800 hrs …the "Standby Call" for all world radio stations, all world news agencies. "Stand by for an important announcement by the Supreme Allied Commander, General Dwight D. Eisenhower!" Clear and distinct came the words from the IKE, even the three little words. Within five minutes we had "clear reception" reports from London, from Washington. Then a few minutes later another type of report ... the irate voice over unclear telephone wires of Bedell Smith, Chief of Staff to Eisenhower: "What in hell were we trying to do????"

Disaster. The duplicate disk had been turned over to the disk jockey without comment, play at 1800 hrs. following "Will now hear the voice of the Supreme Commander General Dwight D. Eisenhower … then nothing but garbled goobly goop! The jockey, realizing the trouble ... "Due to technical difficulties the announcement of the Supreme Commander will be read in a few moments."

A mere technical error. The original recording of the IKE had been made at so-called amateur speed, and the unsuspecting jockey had played the disc at "pro" speed.

Together with plaudits from the world for clearness, speed, and accuracy, we also got hell from the High Brass.

Moral: Don't Gild the Lily!

7. MARCH MURDERS

Twenty-five-year-old Austrian, Lola Fredericks, was elated over her new position as Secretary to the Director of the famed Vienna Park Hotel Schoenbrunn, for the last year occupied by transient officers and families of the British Occupational Forces, Austria. In one corner of her office, "Lumpie," a sky-blue paroquet, drowsed in his cage while his dutiful mate watched carefully over two tiny eggs. The daily accounts had been balanced. Herr Director Kortofsky and the British military hotel manager had just departed. Outside in the Grand Salon there was music of Viennese waltzes as English and Austrian guests danced, laughed and gaily flirted. In the apartments directly above the hotel office were three tiny babies, peacefully asleep in their cribs. It was 10:25 p.m., March 19, 1946, and all was well with blonde Lola, unknowing and uncaring about strife-torn Palestine, and war-worried Europe.

Ten seconds later Lola's body was a torn mass of flesh.

From the densely packed bar adjoining the hotel office came screams as knife-like bits of glass pierced through human bodies. From upstairs, cries of tiny babies, rudely awakened by the searing bite of glass fragments … all following a thunderous blast that shattered windows and ripped partitions. There was a moment of silence, then sirens, police whistles, British uniformed troopers, Austrian police, and ambulances.

Somewhere out in the darkness, somebody silently laughed in mad joy, someone yet unknown who in darkness had placed a death-laden bomb alongside the unguarded hotel wall. In some strange way – some mad fantasy – that shattering blast with a rush of air driven like a giant hammer to crush everything in its path, had been revenge – revenge for something .... for Palestine against the British … against anyone that could even live in a British hotel.

The fruits of revenge ... the victims ... the torn body of an Austrian girl ... two blue-feathered paroquets ... glass-cut babies ... English soldiers carrying out their assigned duties in a land far removed and unconnected with problems of Arabs or Jews.

Police are investigating, but Lola, unknowing of rights or wrongs of racial strife between nations, is dead.

The toll: one dead, three severely wounded, twenty-one lightly wounded.

At liberty: one terrorist murderer.

* * * * * * * *

8. LEAKAGE

The "Leakage" – It has been going for centuries.

One of WWII's best-kept secrets was the landing of Allied Forces in North Africa, under Gen. Eisenhower, at 1:00 a.m. November 8, 1942. Information that large convoys were steaming from several departure points in US and UK in the direction of Gibraltar was impossible to conceal from the active German air force and sub force, but exact destination was another matter. However, stage magician-like moves keeping attention on the wrong hand were deliberate "leaks."

Potential landing areas in North Africa ranged from Dakar on the Atlantic to Algiers in the Mediterranean, all under control of Vichy France, operating under German Armistice Command at Casablanca. Chief Theo Auer, rabid Nazi. Don Coster, former advertising exec, was captured while driving for the American Ambulance Service in France. He was later released and returned to the USA.

Joining the Navy, drafted, was Wild Bill Donovan of the OSS for a special job in Casablanca, under cover of American consul to Vichy France. Here he encountered two young Austrians who had joined the Foreign Legion to be later interned. In Casablanca they avoided arrest by furnishing information to German Armistice Commission. Coster arranged to supply them with minor information for transmittal and established himself as a minor consular official … young, friendly, big-mouthed, and drunk. Austrians by supplying info to Gen. Auer, minor but easily verified, built up his confidence in information given by drunken Coster that the invasion area was Dakar on the West Atlantic Coast. Immediate word was sent to German naval authorities, so a monster pack of 100 subs were sent to patrol the area.

It was night, Nov. 7. 42 ohms German radio flashed news that large Allied convoys were sighted off Gibraltar, headed for North Africa, a mere 2000 miles from Dakar. Long leak!

Mixed Brit and Free French forces under De Gaulle made an abortive attempt to invade North Africa at Dakar, Sept. 24, 1940. The operation was planned by ex-monk Capt. G. Thierry D'Argentlieu, C/S to De Gaulle. He badly mishandled it, with two cruisers hit including Jean Bart, losing prestige for the Free French.

The attitude of the Vichy French toward the African invasion was also doubtful, despite efforts by Bob Murphy, American Consul to North Africa, who, however succeeded in getting information from high French Officers as to Casablanca, Algiers, Oman, and Tunis… French Navy plans to prevent landings … where French resistance would be tough, or token.

This information was given to Gen. Clark, heading the US mission. The only leak in this case was when the small boat capsized, losing Clark's pants.

9. THE MAKING OF A SPY

I have been informed that giving birth to an infant child is no particular feat. I have also been informed otherwise. But the following incident, involving giving birth to a full grown and full blown master spy is an entirely different proposition. This was the case with Mark U. Hamilton-Fourby.

It was a quiet Sunday afternoon on the beach of the Allied Press camp near Algiers. Escaping from the heat and noise of the city, the confusion of the Hotel Alletti and its adjacent "Snake Pit," the faint, miasmic fragrance from the romantic Kasbah nearby, a number of representatives of the journalistic profession relaxed in the sparkling waters of the Mediterranean, later to gather for a beach supper around a driftwood fire, food washed down by flagons of local Algerian wine supplemented by the local Eau de Vie.

The initial thrill and interest of the island attacks on Lampedusa, Pantelleria, and Sicily had slowly died down with the slow movement of the Allied forces across the major island. Monty [General Montgomery], had pushed past Catania, the scene of furious paratroop battles, and was methodically plodding northward, his main obstacle being an elaborate series of land mines. Bradley was going the hard way directly across the island, taking one ridge of fortified hills, only to be faced with another. Georgie Patton had just started to roll on his famous end run around Palermo. Everything was going according to plan … nobody had been slapped … no donkeys had been shot. Monty had even permitted coughing at his press conference. Things were dull, almost boring.

Someone, I think it was Joe Phillips, one of my star propaganda advisors and formerly of *Newsweek*, started bemoaning the fact that war was no longer an individual effort, even along spy lines … no World War II Mata Hari. In fact, the international spy racket seemed to be on the decline. This idea was more or less agreed to by the gathering.

But with a few more flagons of Algiers' best, the spirit of initiative suddenly arose. "No spies? We'll provide one!!!"

A veritable flood of suggestions as to type, as to name. There was a unanimous decision that he should be a renegade Guardsman, bitter at dismissal from the service, which gave rise to a rather British combination of names: Mark U. Hamilton Fourby. The first portion came from an incident related in England during the bombing period when only absolutely necessary travel was permitted. As a consequence, a young newly married couple had to forego the usual honeymoon trip and remain at home. The following morning, the young brother of the bride, who had closely observed the action through a large keyhole, wrote his boyhood friend along the following lines:

"And mark you, Hamilton, this type of behavior from a girl that told me only yesterday that to blow my nose in public was most impolite!"

The Fourby portion came from a British wartime club – the four B's: Bridge, Badminton, Beer, and Bed. The newly created Master-Spy – Mark U. Hamilton-Fourby!

With an accepted name and a created personage, the developing procedure was simple for career journalists, and Hamilton-Fourby's creators were the elite: Ernie Pyle; Helen Kirkpatrick; Johnnie Knickerbocker; John Thompson; Wes Gallagher, now AP Chief; Charlie Daly – later John Charles Daly (CBS); Noel Monks, Australian journalist and former husband of Mary Monks Lewis (later Mrs. Hemmingway); and Quent Reynolds of *Colliers,* whose London blitz stories did more to help England than all the BBC output. Tacit permission was given enabling birth announcements and exploits to pass censorship by Lt. Col. Scott-Bailey, my chief of Censorship.

There was a rumored resemblance in action to Lawrence of Arabia: conflicting descriptions – medium-sized, brown hair, capable of instant change by a master of disguise, a talented linguist speaking all major tongues and innumerable dialects, an expert shot with small arms, fencer extraordinaire, black-belt judo expert and a board-splitting karate chop in either hand, above all a smiling inoffensive face that could suddenly flame to a mask of livid hatred. It took time and considerable development before it was clearly established on which side he was serving. His various originators had different ideas as to his supposed intentions and feelings. From his demonstrated ability to play single agent, double agent and occasional triple agent roles, Hamilton-Fourby became a problem and a worry to both Allied and Axis counter-intelligence experts.

Rumors from the Mid-east tied Hamilton-Fourby in with the Axis butler in Cairo, who photographed everything from the ultra secret papers of the British Ambassador to some of his gayer intimate garments. An almost authentic report had him placed in the Vatican until it was shown that the man suspected was a member of the Swiss Guard, who, when off-duty, wore high-button shoes, a favorite footgear of the master spy.

At our small mess in Algiers, Villa Brossette, slightly removed from Hotel St. George, the supreme headquarters, were usually four British and four American officers – one being, invariably, the Chief of Staff.

A British mess-mate, Col. Hill-Dillon, was Chief of Counter Intelligence, which gave me a wonderful chance to pass along the various alleged exploits of Hamilton-Fourby. For awhile I got no particular reaction but then suddenly I was approached by Hill-Dillon: "McChrystal, old chap, I think you press fellows are being done in by that Fourby fellow. In the first place he is an impostor. We have definitely established that he never was a member of the Brigade of Guards as claimed. There are a few Fourbys, but absolutely no Hamilton-Fourby. But, we're giving him a bit of rope, and he'll tangle his loop, as you Americans have it!"

Then, like everything else, even Hamilton-Fourby faded from public interest. Sicily was over; Patton had slapped and been chewed out, but the story was still untold, as the Germans thought that he was poised with his complete army ready to hit the soft Axis underbelly. Rommel had gotten the bulk of his soldiers across Messina Straits. The Italians had surrendered, and Clark had landed at Salerno.

Hamilton-Fourby's last activity was reported as white slave traffic in Tangiers and the combined group of origin felt that he should be given a final fling in Algiers. The word of his coming was quietly passed around and a hint given that he would be willing to talk, under proper conditions and with intelligence people of influence. This informational gem dropped casually and intentionally, hit the eager ears of Commander Harry Butcher, ADC to the "Ike" and Vice President, on leave, of the Columbia Broadcasting System. Like the majority of aides, Butch was an "eager beaver" type and his enthusiasm knew no bounds.

Several days later arrangements were complete. Johnnie Thompson, mid-western journalist, had spent so much time and money in a small bar hidden away in the depths of the Kasbah that he was entrusted with all interior arrangements. It was 2:00 a.m., when Butch, Joe Phillips and myself stood outside the heavy iron door leading to the bar. After a series of pre-arranged knocks and a muttered challenge, we were then admitted into the dim-lit confines of the establishment. Rag wicks in hanging bowls of bean oil gave out slight illumination, and the odor of burnt oil, garlic and plain sweat gave a distinct atmosphere. On one side were several uniformed war correspondents, and in a dim corner, flanked on each side by an armed guard, stood a small figure, clad in an enveloping burnoose.

There was absolute silence as Butcher approached the group. In his best CBS Vice-Presidential tone, "Hamilton-Fourby, I presume! I am Commander Butcher, representing the Supreme Commander!"

There was a stiff bow and acknowledgement in somewhat broken English. The ADC glanced at a list of prepared questions, then started an interrogation of the spy: what were his impressions of the current campaign, relative merits of the opposing forces and groups, impression of leaders –Eisenhower, De Gaulle, Leclerc, Paget, Rommel…

It was noted that the spy's answers to various questions were exceedingly brief, at times almost inaudible. A surprise, considering Fourby's reputation as a linguist. It seemed as if he were suffering from some sort of speech impediment. Even in the dim light one could see facial contortions. Finally he threw back his head … out came a shout of laughter … and three small pebbles!

Simultaneously, overhead electric lights flashed on, clearly revealing the two confronting characters – Commander Harry Butcher, U.S. Navy; Aide; and CBS Vice-President, Mark U.; Hamilton-Fourby, Master Spy, alias Charlie Daly, CBS war correspondent (later John Charles Daly, ''What's My Line'').

For a moment Butch was speechless, then a muttered, "You damn little bastard, I'll fire you for… A quick set of his jaw … a grin, forced, but a grin. "Alright, all you bastards, I'm buying!!!"

The little Kasbah bar did a record-breaking business the night when Hamilton-Fourby ceased to exist. But his memory stayed on.

Whenever there was a bad foul-up, press wise or otherwise, Fourby did it!

10. Medals, Anyone?

Over the centuries ornamentation has served to distinguish outstanding individuals from the common herd. In olden days an enemy nose or set of ears, or even a complete head marked the wearer as a person to be noted, especially indoors in hot weather. This type of decoration proving unwieldy, the trend shifted to bits of shiny metal tied together with rope or ribbon – the basis of today's medals and campaign badges.

Medals can be awarded for superior performance in many fields – heroism, efficiency, and conduct are only a few. I recall during WWII in North Africa there was a medal presented to visiting firemen and other dignitaries by the Sultan at Marrakech – a dingy blob of brass, and the ribbon a jaundiced yellow with red bumps. The decoration as I understood it, was the "Order of Tizzi Uzu." Several years later, while in Washington, I happened to mention this particular decoration and was taken quietly aside by a friend, originally schooled as a rabbi and a specialist in Arabic.

"Art," he queried, "Do you know the Arabic characters for that order you just mentioned?" When I replied in the negative he sketched out several characters that seemed familiar, then gave me a rough translation. It seems that "tizzi," as pronounced, means "bottom" and "uzu," a "court." It appears possible that, through a dash of sly Arabic humor, there are many multi-ribboned chests wearing the insignia of "Courtly Posteriors." I sincerely hope not, but it would be funny, wouldn't it?

My original interest in medals was purely along forensic lines. All Hallows College, a boarding school I attended in Salt Lake City, had a yearly elocution contest .... the prize, a shiny gold medal. Considering that I was then operating a handicap of a voice that cracked at critical moments, my winning of the coveted trophy for two years straight was a triumph for my speaking ability, amplified by the drama of Paul Revere's Midnight Ride and the grief of Mudville citizens when the mighty Casey whiffed the third one. The school also gave gold medals for scholarship, but I was satisfied with silver ones, as my midnight oil supply was always short.

It was not until early 1917 when the US jumped into the "War to End All Wars" and I had become a 2nd Lieutenant of Infantry that I began to visualize rows of ribbons adorning my uniform blouse. As a member of the 8th Regular Army Division I was most hopeful. However, "Black Jack" Pershing had had an old time hassle with "Daddy" Morrison, Division Commander, so we fought the Battle of Camp Fremont, California, with a few skirmishes with local girl schools. At war's end, I had a row of silver chevrons plus the WWII Victory Medal, unspoiled by stars or bars, small change in later discussions with gold-chevroned, verbally blood-spattered overseas returnees.

By 1921 my medal expectancy was at all time low when I was ordered to join the US Forces China, a powerful force of some 700 officers and men of the 15th Infantry, stationed at Tientsin, China for the purpose of "keeping the railway open from Peking to the sea," which line had been without trouble for some 21 years. Basically the area did not seem to be a prolific source of military decorations, as the only fighting was the annual civil war between Chang Tso Lin, Warlord of the North, and Wu Bei Fu, Warlord of Central China.

These wars were fought strictly according to tradition. Chang would wait until early Spring, then move south, using the government railways to transport his warriors to the battle area, located some 250 miles south of Tientsin. Then he turned the equipment over to Wu, less a few locomotives needed for preparing tea from their hot water boilers. Both sides wore the standard Chinese gray uniform, felt boots, baggy wrap-around trousers, wrap leggings and a hooded coolie jacket plus an umbrella, as all fighting was supposed to stop with rain. The Chang boys wore a red arm band, the Wu troops a yellow one, and the smart ones carried one of each.

Fighting was not particularly deadly, due to ammunition. After the Russo-Jap War of 1905 stocks of Russian ammunition were stored near Tsingtao, subject to Allied check and control. There were a few scandals when it was discovered that only the towering front row of cases remained in many of the warehouses, the balance having been sold by the back way to various warlords. Meantime the ammunition had so deteriorated that a cartridge would only explode if the rifle was held upright and jammed down on the shoulder, allowing the remaining bits to rest against the firing cap – noisy but inaccurate. Artillery ammunition wasn't much better, but louder.

Chang's troops would invariably be defeated and would retire northwards along the railroad towards Tientsin, slowly followed by Wu. The main duty of the Allied Forces was to shunt the warriors away from the foreign concession areas.

Presence of foreign troops in North China started with the Relief of Peking, following the Boxer Rebellion of 1900, with US, British, French, Japanese, German, Russian, Italian and even Austrian troops remaining until end of WWI, when German, Austrian and Russian holdings were given up. Remaining were the 15th US Infantry and Marine Guard at Peking, British "Loyal Lancs" Regiment, French native Annamite troops, Japanese, and an occasional Italian gunboat from Taku.

Another tradition in the set-up was that the Jap forces would invariably have a senior officer, ranking the US commander, who, nevertheless, would be in full charge of the combined operations shunting Chinese troops around the foreign concessions.

Here was my first real chance for a medal. Following a successful Operation "Shuntaround" the Japanese Adjutant General came to me with a proposal that if the Japanese Commander was to receive any kind of a commendatory letter from Colonel Martin, US Commander, in connection with the operation, he would assure that Colonel Martin and his staff would receive the "Order of the Rising Sun 1st Class" – a shiny neck-hanging job with a brilliant red ribbon.

As Operations Officer, my plan was devious and involved the Colonel's fondness for golf. When he arrived several months before, his only spare baggage was a saber – no golf clubs. Immediate action was taken. A finance clerk, an ex-golf pro, was selected to give him special attention and there was never a more attentive pupil. 1:00 p.m. was a fixed starting time for his weekly match against Consul-General Kerr, British – both contestants shooting an approximate 140. At 12:00 I came to the Colonel's desk, laden with papers for his signature. He started signing, glancing at the clock, then disaster. I had prepared a most non-committal letter to the Japanese General with vague reference to Operation Shuntaround. My mistake. I had put the letter on his personal stationary, off size and off color from the regular. He started to sign, glanced and looked up.

"McChrystal!" he barked, "What the hell is all this about?" I quietly remarked it was merely a commendatory note, just good international relations.

"International relations, my ass!" he exploded as he ripped the letter in half. "Let the other stuff go until Monday. I'll miss my starting time as it is.

So went the Rising Sun 1st Class, due to off-size stationery and a golf starting time. Possibly just as well. I would have had to turn it in after Pearl Harbor anyway.

A later Chang-Wu war gave me another chance. After being defeated and passing by Tientsin, Chang would wait a week or so past Tongshan, center of the coal industry, British owned Kailan Mining Corporation. Chang would regroup before retreating through the Great Wall at Shanikwan and Wu would follow very gingerly. During this particular war I became an Allied Commander with a powerful force of two squads of US soldiers and a company of British Sihks, under a Subadar Major. My orders were to proceed to the Tongshan area and take position between the rival forces, with written instructions. I quote, "Do not bring on an engagement unless absolutely necessary to save life" and "safeguard foreign property.". My Indian vocabulary was seven words – water, food, ammunition, come, go, yes, no – but with Subadar Singh I didn't need any more.

With the rival forces dug in along the railway line about ten miles apart, my main duty was to travel between the opposing lines in my "Special Train" – a locomotive with a freight car front and back – and an Honor Guard, a squad from each nation, saluting on every possible occasion. I was informed by a Chinese interpreter that General Wu had recommended me for a Chinese decoration – Order of the Golden Fleece. When I inquired as to when and where this high honor was to be bestowed, the interpreter informed me that the medal was temporarily out of stock and no funds available unless I would provide the cost – some $120.00 US currency. Being a little short of cash, I settled for a citation in Chinese.

Many years went by before another special medal situation arose. As a retired major, I was living peacefully in San Francisco when recalled to duty in October, 1940, as a political advisor to "Uncle Joe" Kennedy, then Ambassador to the Court of St. James, London. He was apparently a little bit worried about the Germans and my appointment could have been a final straw. He immediately left England with his entire family. I remained in England with Ambassador Winant, and I finally got my second American Medal – The Freedom Medal, designed to make draftees happy about the first draft in peacetime. The special situation arose with Pearl Harbor. Apparently thinking only of this event, the War Department issued a Special Regulation, authorizing one battle star with the medal for each hostile action undergone, dating back to the original date of issue of the medal. Here was a great opportunity. In a carefully documented and prepared letter to the War Department, presenting positive evidence of being under 469 hostile actions during the period concerned

– Goering's Luftwaffe were certainly not paying friendly visits. My query, thinking of the battle stars – do I wear a sash or a girdle? It took several months before I received a reply from the Adjutant General, inviting my attention to changes in Special Regulations, limiting battle stars to one for the medal concerned. However, it was a good try.

11. THE 17-MINUTE SURRENDER

A British Army regulation, a general's stomachache, a slightly illegal operation and a search for a longhaired dachshund all played parts in the months-long happenings and operations leading to the surrender of the Axis armies in northern Italy of 1,600,000 officers and men that was signed April 29, 1945, to be effective May 2, in Caserta, Italy, in the headquarters of Allied Forces Mediterranean Theater.

For three months there had been vague, uncertain whispers, rumors and suggestions with participants and allegiances varying widely. Some of the cast were Allen Dulles, espionage chief for "Wild Bill" Donovan of the Office Strategic Services, in Bern, Switzerland; Field Marshall Sir Harold Alexander, Supreme Commander Allied Forces at Caserta; Signor Pirelli, Italian rubber magnate, anxious to resume tire manufacturing; churchmen desirous that churchly treasures be spared, and Swiss Professor Russman convinced further destruction was a waste.

On the German side, Adolf Hitler's ambassador to Italy had changed sides. While Heinrich Rimmler, the Gestapo and SS chief, toyed with the idea of working with Count Folke Bernadotte of Sweden, Gen. Karl Wolff, SS chief for Italy, realized the game was over.

In February, Dulles' assistant, Gero Gaevernitz, had been contacted by Pirelli and Russman with a vague surrender proposal, mostly important for its mention of possible German Army supporters: Gen. Friedrich Dollman and Capt. Zimmer, of the SS, supposedly influential with Wolff. Ritter von Paul, Air Chief for Italy, also was reported to be interested. Difficulty was the personal oath of fealty to Hitler sworn to by all German high command officers except those of the SS.

Then came word from Dulles that he had met with Wolff, Dallman, and Zimmer, besides Wolff's adjutant, Maj. Wenner. They had discussed generalities and conditions, incidentally learning that Field Marshall Kesselring was favorable. This brought about plans to have my mess-mate, Maj. Gen. Terrence Airey, G-2, and Maj. Gen. Lyman Lemnitzer, longtime special U.S. adviser to Alexander, visit Dulles in Switzerland for the announced purpose of purchasing a special type of long-haired dachshund.

Construction also was started on a small guest house on the hill over the Royal Palace near our small headquarters mess and the Kennels, the abode of Alexander and his personal staff.

At this critical period, I discovered Airey frantically chewing painkiller pills purchased from the British NAAFI exchange and worrying about his appendix. When I asked him why he didn't report to the hospital, he replied glumly that British regulations made absence from duty for more than six weeks cause for reduction from wartime to peacetime rank and he didn't intend starting out again as a lieutenant colonel. So he was quickly and successfully separated from his appendix by a cooperative U.S. surgeon.

Lemnitzer and Airey soon were on their dachshund search, meeting also with Dulles in Ancona. There he was discussing with Wolff and party the surrender requirements and the possibility of influencing other high German officers, despite the fealty oath. Lemnitzer brought a proposal from Alexander that if qualified representatives could come to Switzerland with a bona fide surrender proposal he would guarantee safe passage to Caserta and return.

With signs of peace came unexpected trouble and bad news. Dulles had reported his meetings to the Combined Chiefs of Staff in Washington. With childlike trust, they repeated the entire gist of the meeting to Moscow. It hit the Russian political fan! Wild charges by Stalin of "double crossing by Roosevelt" and "special one-sided agreements" were hurled. To add to the complexity, President Roosevelt died April 12, and relations between Russia and the Allies, especially the U.S., deteriorated further.

On the German side, Dulles learned from Pirelli that Wolff was in trouble with Rimmler and Dr. Ernst Kaltenbrunner, of the SS, over the Bern trip, and Kesselring had been transferred to the Western Front, replaced by nonpolitical Gen. Heinrich von Vietinghoff.

A final blow came on April 21 in the form of a directive from the Combined Chiefs ordering that "all contacts leading towards peace will be immediately stopped." Further we were ordered to inform Moscow of all moves through Gens. Dean and Archer in Moscow.

Word from Dulles was that Gen. Wolff, Capt. Wenner and Lt. Col. Victor von Schweinitz, representing Gen. von Vietinghoff, were on their way to Bern and were prepared to proceed to Caserta to arrange for the surrender of all Axis troops in Italy.

Alexander immediately messaged the Combined Chiefs to lift the stop order plus another to Dulles to stall the Germans until word could be received from the Combined Chiefs.

I was directed by the field marshal to arrange press and photo coverage. He gasped slightly when I requested six correspondents plus a 10-man photo team from my Rome office. One difficulty was interesting the six correspondents in the supposed checking over ancient archives at Caserta, the cover story.

Early on the 27th came a triple-priority message lifting all stops and directing Alexander to proceed with negotiations. Also that a Russian officer would be present at the signing. Dulles was informed of the lifting and directed to send envoys to Caserta the afternoon of the 28th. Meantime, Wolff had returned to Balzano, fearful that von Vietinghoff would weaken.

Around 2 p.m. a small plane with dim markings and flashing special recognition signals landed at the closed Caserta airfield. Three civilian-clad passengers were carried away to the newly-built guest house, where they were presented with a 30-page surrender document and informed that a Russian officer would be present at the signing. The next meeting at 9 p.m. proved to be an all-night session between the Germans and Gaevernitz, Lemnitzer, and Airey. Von Schweinitz outlined Gen. von Vietinghoff's wishes as to surrender formalities. Another request was that von Vietinghoff's Army C would be held intact to maintain camp order and possibly maintain order in Germany.

Maj. Wenner announced his full willingness to sign, but von Schweinitz did not feel his authorization would cover all points, so a message was sent von Vietinghoff at Balzano at 4 a.m., April 29, asking for immediate reply and full agreement. Minor changes were inserted and the envoys were in formed that signing would be in the afternoon to enable them to return to Balzano via Switzerland by the following day.

My correspondents' and photo team's interest quickened when all were summoned to the office of the chief of staff, Lt. Gen. William Morgan, and briefed. The photo team started rigging lights, cables and cameras, but paused as Alexander entered the office and smiled. "Looks like Hollywood, McChrystal," he remarked and disappeared into his private office. A pooled story, releasable noon Greenwich Time, May 2, was already prepared, and at 1:50 p.m. selected spectators were admitted and placed. At 2 p.m., it was cameras ready! After three months of frustration and planning for 17 minutes of action, the order was "Roll."

Down the long entrance hall leading to Gen. Morgan's office came a group of five, the German envoys Schweinitz and Wenner in civilian clothes, Gens. Lemnitzer and Airey, followed by Gaevernitz.

As the Germans approached the end of the hall, there was a glare of lights and flash bulbs. For a moment there was a startled look and then the two envoys moved stiffly and impassively to indicated places at the end of a long table. At the other end, flanked by two members of the secretariat, stood Gen. Morgan, holding in his hand a sheaf of documents. Close behind a row of Allied officers, including Adm. Alan Kirk, Gens. Lemnitzer and Airey, a colonel from the staff of Gen. Mark Clark, a Russian officer, his name still unknown, and myself, stage manager for the day. Behind were six war correspondents and the photo team – 30 men in all – witnessing the first surrender of Axis troops in northern Italy and southern Austria. Personally, I think the correct count was 31. The additional witness looked through a one-way mirror in the door of Alexander's private office.

No bows, no salutes, no greetings. Gen. Morgan, looking directly at the Germans, spoke in low, measured tones. Gen. Morgan explained the terms were to take effect by noon GMT, May 2nd.

Five copies of the approximate 30-page document were laid out for signing. Before signing, von Schweinitz commented that he was going beyond his authorization with the assumption that Gen. von Vietinghoff would accept same. There was a look of dismay from some observers, but from Gen. Morgan a firm "I accept."

In exactly 17 minutes the envoys had left the room accompanied by Gaevernitz – no bows, no farewell salutations. Lights faded as the documents were delivered to Alexander's office. Seventeen short minutes culminating months of frustrating negotiations to bring an already lost war to an end, despite Hitler.

At the last briefing of correspondents by Gen. Morgan, I asked if they would like to see more archives. There were several vulgar replies. We settled for champagne in Gen. Morgan's private office.

The three days from noon GMT, May 2, the effective date of the surrender, were long and worrisome, especially to staffers desirous that their chief, Alexander, get the credit for the first major surrender after the Forgotten Front.

Kesselring on the Western Front asked to whom he could surrender and suggested the announcement be postponed 48 hours so he could get clear of the advancing Russians. Alexander informed Gen. Dwight D. Eisenhower of the suggestion and offered to postpone. Back came a fast message: "You get yours, Alex. I'll get mine later."

The envoys' return was not uncomplicated. They found the Swiss border closed at midnight, and that Gauleiter Hofer, of the Tyrol, had switched and reported Wolff's and von Vietinghoff's actions to Kesselring. Fearing arrest at the border, they traveled in an unmarked car over snow-covered back roads to Bolzano. Meanwhile Hitler had shot himself and Mussolini and his mistress were shot by partisans and hung upside down on a butcher rack in Milan.

Just two hours before the deadline on May 2 came this message from Wolff for Kesselring: "For the sphere of the command of C-in-C Southwest, I subscribe to both the written and oral conditions of the armistice agreement."

Guns were still in Italy for the first time, six long days before the end of World War II in Europe, May 8, 1945.

Originally published byVeterans of Foreign Wars (VFW), May 1980, reprinted here with permission.

12. MICHIE RAN A BAR

Michie ran a bar. She was also a countess and a terrific character. In the rather quiet days following World War II, the village of Mondsee was only known for the fact that it was sited on the shores of Mondsee and nearby was Schloss Mondsee, property of the Almeida family, plus an ancient Catholic cathedral.

It was Michie who perceived the attraction of having a first-class eating and drinking establishment near the lake and also near the autobahn running between Salzburg and Vienna. The family Schloss provided the answer.

Furniture was brought down from the vast rooms and corridors of the castle. Bright gay colors decorated the large downstairs rooms leading from the massive entrance hall. A small kitchen was installed, together with an extensive bar. With Michie at the helm, both as supervisory cook and mixer, the Castillo Bar became an instant success, drawing from hotels of Salzburg and from the heavy autobahn traffic.

There was another business venture connected with the Schloss Mondsee. This was the usage of series of first floor rooms by Herr Jeager, running an antique shop with features from furniture to rugs. It was successful, including with the public.

It was a quiet Fall afternoon and Herr Jeager decided to break some personal news that, to the time, had only been known by his very definite boyfriend. He sent the boyfriend down to the Castillo Bar to request the company of owner Michie for a special announcement. Michie appeared, together with a special bottle of Scotch. However after she had poured drinks all around, the news came. Herr Jeager made the announcement of his engagement to an American widow, who was also on her way to Mondsee. Michie immediately shoved the cork back in the scotch bottle and departed.

There was a decided coolness, further cooled by the arrival of the US widow and the ice and snow of winter. The widow snugly, ensconced in Schloss Mondsee, took a rather dim view of the boyfriend until assured that he was merely an old retainer.

A further rough spot developed when Jeager suggested that a sizeable portion of the widowly money be shipped to a Swiss bank to avoid undue taxes. This proposal was met by the widow with a statement to the effect that her husband had made his money in the United Sates of America and she was not going to be a party to any move to deprive Uncle Sam of his legitimate portion. During the winter and early spring the only heated things around Schloss Mondsee were the arguments between Jeager and widow, who, draped in full flannel underwear, repeated her financial beliefs.

But Spring, with gay flowers and warming breezes, finally arrived, as did the formal wedding at the Mondsee cathedral, attended by a heavy sprinkling of somewhat destitute nobility, glad of a free meal and drinks, especially at the Castillo Bar, whose owner Michie had easily forgiven. The dowry was finally paid and the entire ménage Jeager, ex-widow, boyfriend and Michie joined in a swank bridal trip to Spain.

But all the excitement and novelty of the situation proved too much for the ex-widow, who romantically expired, leaving the entire property to Jeager, who in turn put the boyfriend into a commanding position.

It was almost a year later when Michie and Jeager came into the Hotel Bristol for a cocktail before attending a major dinner party. Michie, beautifully clad, looked her best, and the management under Pieto the bartender's service, did their best to contribute to the gayety.

Gay it was as Michie and Jeager departed for the dinner. Late that evening came the sad news that at the dinner Jaeger had choked to death while eating. This was a saddening affair, made much sadder some weeks later when the Jeager Will was read, giving his entire estate to the boyfriend.

13. THE CANADIAN SAFARI

Our recent [early 1970's] tour of the Canadian Pacific Hotels in Canada was primarily due to Adolph Hitler and his favorite haunt, Berchtesgaden, Germany. With the end of WWII this area became an Armed Forces Recreation Center, and young Don Curtis, war veteran, started his meteoric career as a hotel operative with his first job as Manager of Hotel Berchtesgadener Hof, former luxury hotel of Hitler's V.I.P.s. Following my retirement from the Army I became involved in hotel operations in Vienna and Salzburg, Austria, and in developing a fishing club on a wonderful trout stream on the River Traun at Bad Ischl, Austria. As fellow hotel operators Don and I got along splendidly except for basic disagreement over use of spinners instead of flies for the wily trout. While I remained in Austria until the late sixties, Don went steadily ahead: establishing the Steigenburger chain in Germany, Hotel Corporation of America in France, Hotel El Presidente in Johannesburg, and Club Mediterranee, as hotel advisor to banker Guy Rothschild of Paris.

We kept close contact, checking various hotel possibilities, and about two years ago he asked my advice on two newly offered positions: Presidency of a Far-East Hotel chain, and Presidency of Canadian Pacific Hotels, Ltd. My choice to advise him about Canada was not unselfish. I had seen the Orient and had never been to Canada.

Meantime I had withdrawn from active hotel operations and was living quietly at Rancho Carlsbad, near San Diego with my wife Dorothy when an invitation came from Don that we make a small Canadian safari. We had a three-hour flight from San Diego to O'Hare airport, where we circled for another hour, missing the American-Canada connecting flight and landing four hours late at Toronto ... with Don's charming wife, smiling Jill Curtis patiently waiting. We went on to the majestic Hotel Royal York with a reception committee, all young and all hungry ... so were we. It was past midnight when we were escorted to our modest Dutch Suite on the Royal floor, overlooking Lake Ontario. Another pleasant sight: a cluster of roses, a basket of fruit and a bottle of W. Harper. Despite exhaustion, we sampled both fruit and bourbon.

Some Factual Data on Ontario

Ontario is Canada's richest province, with a thousand miles square, a quarter million lakes, wandering streams, evergreen forests and clean air. The islands along the St. Lawrence River abound with beaches and recreational resorts, great fishing and more moose and caribou than in the good old days when John Cabot arrived in Newfoundland. The mineral riches are abundant, with metals including gold, silver, copper and iron with dashes of platinum, palladium, and uranium in the Bancroft area. Nineteen million acres are lush green land.

Thirty thousand peaceful Indians were living in Huronia early in the seventeenth century when some Jesuits moved in seeking souls while their companions were seeking anything loose, especially furs. Sammy Champlain, looking over Southern Ontario, ganged up with the Hurons, Algonquins and Montagnois against the warlike Iroquois. Étienne Brûlé and Jean Nicholet explored the Great Lakes. In jolly England, Prince Rupert, cousin of Charles II, dug up enough schillings to outfit the "Nonesuch" for a voyage to Hudson Bay, the start of the Hudson Bay Company.

Fights over the fur trade led to the Seven Years' War between France and England, resulting in France losing all possessions in North America, except for a couple of small islands. Southern Ontario became part of a vast province, Quebec, now Canada's largest province, four times larger than France from whom it was separated in 1773. Of today's Quebec population of over six million, 82% are of French descent and politically most active and vocal.

In 1791 Upper Canada was created west of the Ottawa River under English rule, becoming Canada West in 1841. In 1867 it became

Ontario, with the capital at Ottawa. Final boundaries were drawn in 1912.

Toronto, originally Fort Rouille and later Fort York, is a bustling city of over two million [now 6,196,731, as of 2020]. You can tour the city, boat ride among Lake Ontario islands, watch a samurai-like Japanese chef do knife tricks at "Benihana of Tokyo," eat poached salmon in the Acadian Room of the York, or try dinner at "Honest Ed's Warehouse," amid thousands of Tiffany lamps. A tourist "must" is a visit to Niagara Falls and the Skylon, a 530-foot revolving tower overlooking Horseshoe Falls. The so-called "Golden Horseshoe" area between Niagara Falls and Oshawa is the center of financial and industrial production, plus the theatre and film industries.

Montreal, Quebec

Thunder Bay is the western terminus of the St. Lawrence Seaway, the geographical center of Canada, with a wilderness stretching to the shores of Hudson Bay. One grain elevator, Saskatchewan #7, stores enough grain to provide a two-pound loaf for everyone in North America. How dull and how fattening!

Montreal – a city of concrete, steel and brass with great underground malls and parking lots, is built on an island with a mountain in the middle. It's quite metropolitan, with more churches (550) than any city in North America, and also more bars. (Note: Did not personally check!). Notre Dame is absolutely beautiful, especially in coloration, while Basilica St. Mary's is a half-size St. Peters. The Laurentians, one of the world's oldest mountain chains, loom south of the Canadian Shield. The range is studded with lakes, streams and valleys unsuitable for cultivation, but great for fishing.

Our first sightseeing was a quick trip down the "Breakneck Stairs," built by Joliet In 1684, connecting the upper and lower levels of the city, then a visit to Notre Dame de Victoire with the altar a perfect replica of an old fort, followed by a ferry ride across the river to Levis (a town, not pants). Finally we went up the Promenade to the Plains of Abraham, site of the famed battle between Wolfe and Montcalm, resulting in the death of both and a French defeat. We were dinner guests at the Officers' Mess of the 22nd Royal Regiment. The club rooms were deep within the massive Citadel walls, with its partitions made from old sailing ship ballast bricks, and the dining table seating fifty made from old ship timbers.

Some Quebec History

Quebec is Algonquin for "narrows," marking the shape of the St. Lawrence at that point. Cartier and other fishermen caught cod, whales and seals around 1535, and Tadaussac founded the first trading post in 1599. The redoubtable Champlain founded Quebec City as a small two-story fort, with small cannons attempting to hold the fur trade against French independents.

Cardinal Richelieu in 1637 organized the Company of New France, agreeing to furnish 200 to 300 settlers in the area in exchange for control of the new government and the fur trade. With France and England at war, settlers were intercepted and, together with Champlain, surrendered and were forced to return to France. Later, Champlain returned to the trading post at Three Rivers, only to die a year later before establishing Montreal.

Then things got really complicated. French military officer, Sieur de Maisonneuve with a gang of workers, two Jesuits plus a few soldiers landed on the island, climbed Mount Royal and founded Villa Marie. The Iroquois recommenced raiding, to be restrained by heroic efforts of Anthony Dillard, but continued for some ten years.

Louis XIV proclaimed New France as a Royal Colony, sending out some 1000 soldiers. In 1667 he signed a peace treaty with the Mohawks, and the Iroquois sought easier pickings to the south. Jean Talon was sent out as "Royal Intendant" to supplement the Governor and started offering large tracts of land to selected persons if they would provide settlers. He helped out by sending 1000 brides. These landowners, designated as "Seigneurs," were required to build a manor house, chaples and mills, and were given judicial rights, while settlers paid rent, usually in produce, and worked four days a year on the owner's land.

But fur trade had more appeal than farming, and a succeeding Governor, Louis de Baude, Compte de Palluau and, de Frontenac backed the fur traders. Coureurs de Bois [an independent French fur trader] disagreed with Intendant Talon. Both were recalled, and the Iroquois with English arms restarted raiding. Frontenac, reappointed in 1689, led the French against New England and the French fur trade was again on top.

During the ensuing seventy years three wars were fought in Europe and North America, while the French explored, established trading posts and forts and the English settled, farmed and moved west. The Plains of Abraham battle between Wolfe and Montcalm marked the start of the British conquest of New France.

In 1760 Montreal fell and a Treaty of 1764 ended French rule in North America. British, American and Scot traders moved to Montreal and joined the French in the fur trade as far as Saskatchewan, displeasing both the English and the American Colonies. During the Revolutionary War, Quebec was invaded by the Americans, who captured Montreal and several towns, to be later driven out.

In 1841 Southern Quebec became Canada East as part of the United Provinces. In 1867 lower Canada became Quebec as part of the Dominion, with present boundaries established in 1912.

The Maritime Provinces, originally called Acadia, were the scene of struggles between French and English since discovery by Sir John Cabot in 1497. A Scot, Sir William Alexander, claimed the discovery and made the area British. The French established a naval base at Louisbourg to defend Quebec, later captured by the British, then returned to France in 1749. Edward Cornwallis founded Halifax the same year. The basis of Longfellow's "Evangeline" was the refusal of the Acadians to take the English loyalty oath.

Following the American Revolution, Loyalists under Sir Guy Carlton moved from New York and settled in Nova Scotia and New Brunswick. Edward Island and Cape Breton, all French-speaking, were also separate, with industries of fishing, lumbering, and shipbuilding.

By 1870 all of the provinces had joined the Confederation.

Originally the fur trade was everything. Verendrye Brothers had trading posts in the 18th century as far west as Portage la Prairie, Manitoba. Captain James Cook was the first European to reach the Pacific in 1778, and in 1791 Captain George Vancouver was sent by England to survey the west coast and to find a route from the Pacific to the Atlantic oceans. The Hudson Bay Company moved inland to establish a post at Saskatchewan River, in competition with the Northwestern Company ("Peddlers from Montreal!"). In 1812 Lord Selkirk of Hudson Bay planted a colony of Scots in the Red River Valley near Winnipeg. After struggles between firms and the French-Canadians, Hudson Bay finally won out and the two firms merged.

David Thompson of Hudson Bay discovered the mouth of the Columbia River. John Jacob Aster's Pacific Fur Co moved into the area but finally gave up. By 1850 Hudson Bay owned all British lands in the west and flatly discouraged settlers.

Then Americans, flooding Oregon territory, demanded annexation by the US to include the Canadian Pacific coast. Their slogan, "Fifty-four Forty or Fight!" was further stimulated by the Fraser Canyon gold rush in 1858. Government bungling was responsible for the Red River Rebellion of the Métis [a polyethnic Indigenous group], under Louis Riel, breaking out in 1869 after Hudson Bay had sold out for one and a half million cash. He wins forty-five thousand acres of land adjoining trading posts.

The Manitoba Act of 1870 finally guaranteed the Métis their land titles, and in 1893 they joined the Federation. The Canadian Pacific Railway was started by Premier McDonald and completed in 1885. Unfortunately another revolt by the Métis under Chiefs Poundmaker and Big Bear was put down by troops, with the hanging of Louis Riel, resulting in the downfall of the McDonald party. The Canadian Pacific Railway and two others finally united in 1917 to form the Canadian National Railway.

Back to The Safari

With Don's return from various travels, we inspected the Royal Floor of the York, the separate apartments for Elizabeth and Philip, private reception room, dining room seating twenty-four guests. We had ice cubes flown In from England, and, during a royal visit, both floors above and below were cleared of guests. On the opposite end is the Governor's Suite, and in the middle, our modest "Butch Suite," tabbed at a mere $150 per day! That night we entertained at the Royal Canadian Military Institute, a typical British club with rules that ladies are only permitted in the dining room and the elaborate "Ladies Lounge"... In the club rooms – Never!

We returned to Montreal by rail and went directly to the airport for our 2300-mile air flight to Calgary. We were expecting a small town, but found a bustling city. Originally established by the Mounted Police to deter whiskey smugglers, Calgary has had an era of wheat farmers and cattle-raising. Now it is the center of the oil industry.

Our flight passed over the provinces of Manitoba, Saskatchewan and half of Alberta. These provinces plus the Northwestern Territories, Yukon and British Columbia comprise Western Canada.

Beginning at the Ontario/Manitoba borders are the Canadian prairies – the Big Sky Country. Yukon and the Northwest Territories extend to within 500 miles of the North Pole, a wilderness of tundra, countless lakes, glacier-clad mountains, sparsely inhabited with three months of warm summer weather and midnight sun. Currently the big thing is oil and oil pipelines.

It was Greyhound Bus this time from Calgary to Banff Springs Hotel, the day brilliant with snow-covered mountains, glaciers and the winding Bow and Elbow Rivers. Our apartment this time was a mere 100 feet long, with a small wet bar, including a view of the Bow Falls and the spectacular Banff Springs golf course. Also the usual flowers, fruit and bourbon. An extra touch was to sit around the outdoor pool, surrounded by glaciers, and watch shapely members of the Canadian girls Olympics squad go through swimming routines.

The next day, we made a short move, by bus, to Chateau Lake Louise, passing big horn sheep, more glaciers, to arrive with the sun still shining on the sparkling lake and on the glaciers.

Dinner was excellent, at a mere seventeen dollars per! Next day, again in bright sunshine, we took a tour of the Columbia ice fields below the Crow Foot Glacier. Halfway to the Athabaska Glacier, the nineteen degree grade was a bit steep for the bus. So we went by foot to the nearby lodge for snow-mobiles to take us over the great expanse of ice-floe over a thousand feet in depth. I had the pleasure of depositing a small miniature bottle of Old Crow in a yawning crevasse – the biggest possible "Bourbon on the Rocks."

Next move, Vancouver, over the Trans-Canadian Highway by bus. We got a far as Kamloops, arriving just in time to see the Canada versus Russian ice-hockey game on TV, together with the entire population. With the spectacular Fraser Canyon and Shuswap Lake coming up, we changed plans the next morning, taking a taxi for the remaining 260 miles. It was and well worth the expense, comfort and fantastic scenery.

We returned home again to Carlsbad after three happy, wonderful weeks, due to Don Curtis, President Canadian Pacific Hotels, Inc.

Arthur J. McChrystal

Brig. Gen. Arthur J. McChrystal, Col. Grogan, Col. Bentley
D-Day at St. Tropez, June 6, 1944

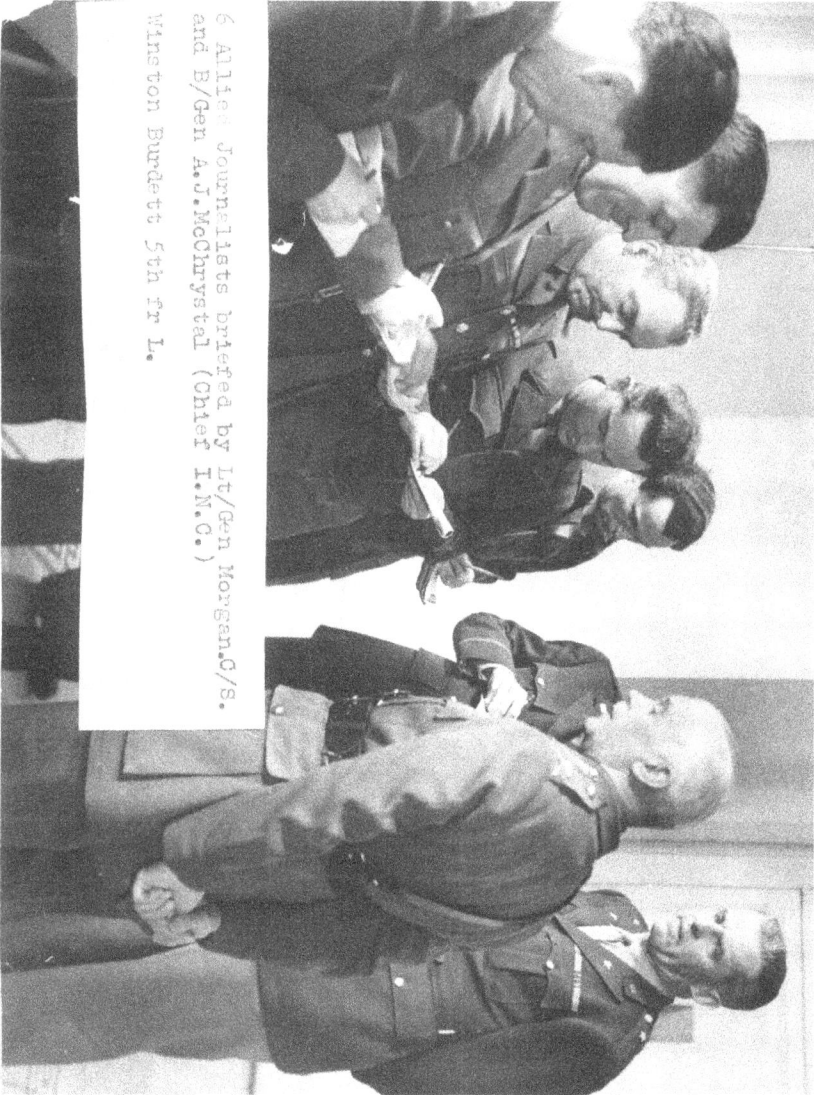

6 Allied journalists briefed by Lt. Gen. Morgan, Combat Support, and Brig. Gen. Arthur J. McChrystal (Chief I.N.C.); Winston Burdet, 5th from left.

Major General Jack Whitley, 1944

M/G Harry Collins   N.Italy '45

Maj. Gen. Harry Collins, No. Italy, 1945

Art (standing in back) and King George of the UK

Hq. Caserta, Italy, 1945, Field Marshal Alexander, Commander, awarding
C.G.E to Arthur J. McChrystal

Actual signing of Surrender by Maj. Werner for SS. Chief Carl Wolff, standing; rear right: Lt. Col. Von Sweinitz

AXIS SURRENDER, April 8, 1956, Caserta, Italy.

Involving N. Italy, So. France, Austria. 1,600,000 men.
Left to Right: Lt. Col Von Sweinitz for Field Marshall Von Wietenhof; Maj. Werner for SS Chief Gen. Carl Wolff. Secretary Gen. Staff, Gaevernitz for Allen Dulles; Brig. Gen. A.J. McChrystal Chief I.N.C.; Adm.Kirk; Lt. Gen. Morgan. Russian officer, Maj. Gen. Lemnitzer; Col. McMillan for Gen. M. Clark; Maj. Gen. Airey.

Major General Walter Schmitt, Algiers, Feb. 11, 1944.
Signed: To Colonel McChrystal, with sincerest good wishes, from his
friend, Walter Schmitt, Major General, U.S.A.

Awd. French Medals Vienna, 1946
Gens. CHERIER, LEWIS, Scoby,
McChrystal, Tate. Col McMillan

(MCCHRYSTAL.. Legion Honor; Croix
de Guerre with Palm)

Art McChrystal awarded the Legion of Honor Croix de Guerre with Palm,
Vienna, 1946. Left to Right: Gens. Gherier, Lewis, Scoby, McChrystal,
Tate, Col. McMillan.

Medals Awarded to Arthur J. McChrystal:
The Brazilian War Medal, Distinguished Service Medal, the Croix de
Guerre with palm, Commander of the British Empire, and an Italian decoration.

Arthur J. McChrystal, above; below: Art in Eureka, Utah, 1915

Art in Eureka, 2013

McChrystal St., Eureka, Utah

Eureka, Utah, 1915

McChrystal St. House in Eureka, Utah, 2013

McChrystal General Merchandise store, 1888

Richard G. McChrystal, Art's grandson, flew P-38 & P-51 fighters, bombed Nazi fighter planes in Europe.

Richard G. McChrystal, May 1943, in front of PT-17 Stearman
primary Trainer, Thunderbird Field, Phoenix, AZ.

Arthur J. McChrystal and son, Richard G. McChrystal, Army Air Force pilot, WWII. Richard flew 71 missions against German fighters and radar-guided flak, while escorting bombers and flying ground patrols.

Arthur McChrystal, civilian, signed, "To Barbara (daugher-in-law) and Dick, (son), Best Wishes, Dad.1956"

Art with McChrystal Grandchildren, Stephen and Karen, Whittier, CA, 1960

Arthur J. McChrystal

Arthur J. McChrystal Biography

Art McChrystal was born in San Jose, California and raised in Eureka, Utah, where his family had extensive mining interests. As a successful mine leasor, he bought half interest in a saloon at sixteen. He received a BS from Stanford in 1915 and an MS in Metallurgy from the University of Utah in 1917. Art was commissioned as 2nd Lt. Infantry Reserve, then Regular Army, following 1st Officers' training camp, May 1917. He served as Athletic Officer, Western Front. He was in the 15th Infantry in China, 1921-25. His travel was extensive: Tibet-Gobi, Manchuria. From 1925-26 he was an instructor in the Infantry School. At Georgia Tech, in 1927, Art coached ends and place kickers for Gill Alexander. At Ft.Thomas, Kentucky, in 1927, he had running prize fights for the Army account. He lived at the Presidio of San Francisco 1928 to 1936.

In 1928 Art originated polo-announcing on the West Coast, to include Del Monte Championships. He went from polo to announcing football, as the "Voice of Kezar Stadium" for 8 years for St Mary's, U.S.F. and Santa Clara, and the Shrine Game. He worked the first pro-football game in west: the Red Grange Galloping Ghost All Stars vs. the College All Stars. Press pundits claimed there was no future for pro-football, no alumni players were able to stand the strain.

On the military side, Art was in charge of the Civilian Conservation Corps (CCC) for 7 Western states from 1932 to 1935, in Washington in 1936, and retired voluntarily as Major in Dec 1937. He was Director of Sports for the San Francisco World's Fair, on Treasure Island, 1939, then later, Director of Amusements and Concessions, plus running two concessions at the Fair.

Oct. 1940 Art was recalled to active duty as political advisor to Ambassador Joe Kennedy in London. Kennedy and family departed prior to his arrival. He remained as Advisor to Ambassador John Winant and Exec. Military Attaché during the Battle of Britain. Then to North Africa with Gen. Eisenhower as Chief of World Press, Censorship and Psychological Warfare for Allied Forces, Mediterranean, serving under Eisenhower and Field Marshals Maitland-Wilson and Alexander until the Axis Surrender in Italy April 28 1945. Next he went to US Forces, Austria, to handle all forms of informational media, including theatre and music. He reopened the Salzburg Music Festival, July 1945. Art founded the *Wiener Kurier,* Aug. 1945, going to 500,000 circulation within 1 year. He founded Austrian Red-White-Red Radio (later TV) network. Art asked to retire as Brigadier General in Dec. 1946.

Returning to Austria, Vienna and Salzbrug in l947, he engaged in public relations and business promotions. In 1950 he married Gretl Hubner, daughter of Hans Hubner, European hotel Magnate. Art started the Hotel Coblenz, Salzburg. He stayed until 1955, when he rebuilt the Hotel Bristol, Salzburg, upon departure of the Allies. It was a most successful operation, with clientele including royalty, prominent people in art, theatre, music and diplomatic circles, as well as the "Sound of Music" cast in 1964.

On the 4.5 mile stretch of the Traun River, in Austria, Art founded the "McTraun Casting and Culture Club," alongside what became one of finest trout streams in Europe.

After the sudden death of his wife in 1968, he returned to the USA. Still unhappy, he returned to Europe via Chapala, Mexico, where he met a charming widow, Dorothy Adkinson, formerly of Long Beach. They were married in 1969. For two years they tried Salzburg in Summer, Chapala in Winter, but found travel too much. So they disposed of the hotel and fishing interests, returned to Mexico, then to the United States for good, trying San Antonio, Tucson, Leisure World at Laguna Hills, and finally Rancho Carlsbad, a perfect home in which to relax, write and enjoy life.

* * *

A CITATION FOR DISTINGUISHED SERVICE

This medal was awarded to ARTHUR J. McCHRYSTAL, Brigadier General, General Staff Corps. Information and Censorship Section, Allied Force Headquarters, for exceptional meritorious service in duty of great responsibility in the Mediterranean Theater of Operations from 13 November 1943 to 18 July 1945. He was Chief of the Information and Censorship Section, Allied Force Headquarters. Brigadier General McChrystal was responsible for all press and radio censorship, military and civil, in the Mediterranean Theater of Operations, and was charged with coordination end executive control of the activities of the Public Relations Officer. In addition to this, he exercised supervision over the Psychological Warfare Branch, Allied Force Headquarters, and supervised its withdrawal from North Africa and subsequent establishment in Italy. From October 1944 to July 1945, Brigadier General McChrystal served as Chairman of the Psychological Warfare Sub-Committee, and was directly responsible to the Chief of Staff for the formulation of its policy. Under his supervision, the Psychological Warfare Branch and Information and Censorship Section of Allied Force Headquarters attained standards of efficiency which resulted in their becoming models of organization for other theaters of war. Brigadier General McChrystal's unique organizational ability, outstanding leadership, unusual tact and spirit of cooperation, together with a wide experience in public relations made him an invaluable member of the Allied Force Headquarters and won him the esteem of war correspondents and British and American officers with whom he came in contact. He entered service from San Francisco, California.

Arthur J. McChrystal

www.ingramcontent.com/pod-product-compliance
Lightning Source LLC
Chambersburg PA
CBHW072009040426
42447CB00009B/1547